T0248223

Why Empires Fall

Why Empires Fall

*Rome, America, and the
Future of the West*

Peter Heather and John Rapley

Yale
UNIVERSITY PRESS
New Haven and London

First published in 2023 in the United States by Yale University Press
and in the United Kingdom by Penguin Books Limited.

Copyright © Peter Heather and John Rapley, 2023
First published by *Penguin Books Limited*.
The moral right of the authors has been asserted.
All rights reserved.

Yale University Press books may be purchased in quantity for educational, business,
or promotional use. For information, please e-mail sales.press@yale.edu (U.S. office)
or sales@yaleup.co.uk (U.K. office).

Typeset in 9.75/13pt Sabon LT Std by Jouve (UK), Milton Keynes.
Printed in the United States of America.

Library of Congress Control Number: 2023933116
ISBN 978-0-300-27372-4 (hardcover : alk. paper)

This paper meets the requirements of ANSI/NISO z39.48-1992 (Permanence of Paper).

10 9 8 7 6 5 4 3 2 1

Contents

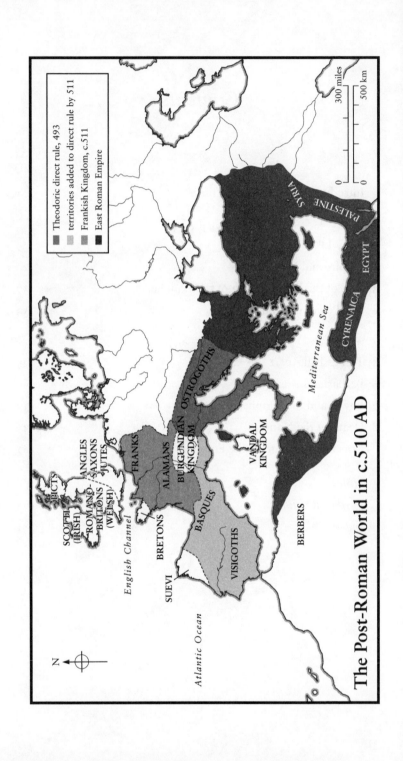

The Post-Roman World in c.510 AD

Theodoric direct rule, 493
territories added to direct rule by 511
Frankish Kingdom, c.511
East Roman Empire

SCOTTI
(IRISH)
PICTS
ANGLES
ROMANO-
BRITONS
(WELSH)
SAXONS
JUTES
FRANKS
ALAMANS
BRETONS
BURGUNDIAN
KINGDOM
OSTROGOTHS
SUEVI
BASQUES
VISIGOTHS
VANDAL
KINGDOM
BERBERS
SYRIA
PALESTINE
EGYPT
CYRENAICA

English Channel
Atlantic Ocean
Mediterranean Sea

300 miles
500 km

N

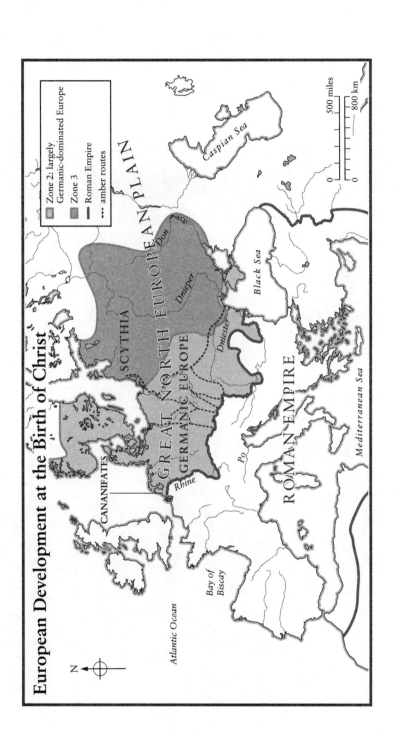

European Development at the "Birth of Christ"

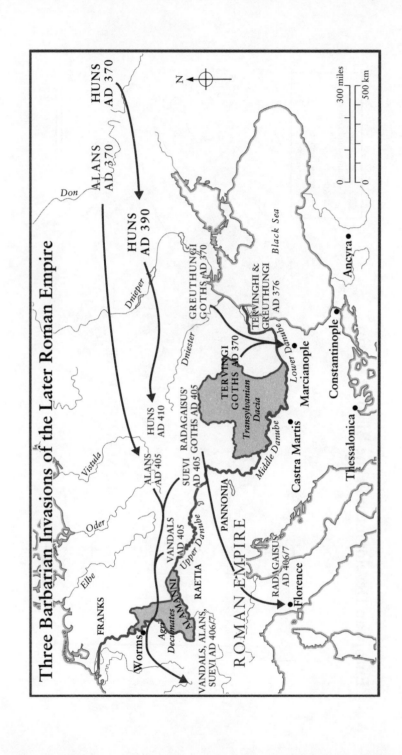

Three Barbarian Invasions of the Later Roman Empire

HUNS AD 370

ALANS AD 370

HUNS AD 390

ALANS AD 370

HUNS AD 410

ALANS AD 405

SUEVI RADAGAISUS' AD 405 GOTHS AD 405

VANDALS AD 405

VANDALS, ALANS, SUEVI AD 406/7

FRANKS

Worms

Agri Decumates

ALAMANNI

RAETIA

PANNONIA

ROMAN EMPIRE

RADAGAISUS' AD 406/7

Florence

Castra Martis

Thessalonica

TERVINGI GOTHS AD 370

Transylvanian Dacia

GREUTHUNGI GOTHS AD 370

TERVINGHI & GREUTHUNGI AD 376

TERVINGHI GOTHS AD 376

Marcianople

Constantinople

Ancyra

Black Sea

Don

Dnieper

Dniester

Vistula

Oder

Elbe

Upper Danube

Middle Danube

Lower Danube

N

300 miles

500 km

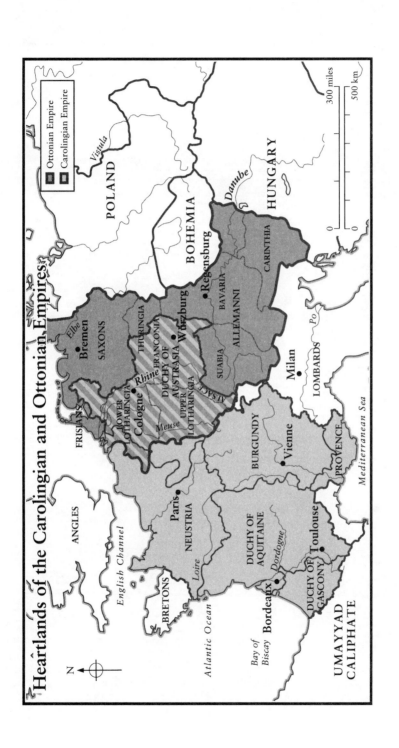

Heartlands of the Carolingian and Ottonian Empires

Ottonian Empire
Carolingian Empire

300 miles
500 km

N

POLAND

Vistula

BOHEMIA

Danube

HUNGARY

Regensburg

CARINTHIA

Elbe

Bremen

SAXONS

THURINGIA

Würzburg

BAVARIA

FRANCONIA

DUCHY OF
AUSTRASIA

ALLEMANNI

Rhine

LOWER
LOTHARINGIA

Cologne

UPPER
LOTHARINGIA

ALSACE

SUABIA

Meuse

Milan

FRISIANS

BURGUNDY

LOMBARDS

Po

ANGLES

Vienne

PROVENCE

English Channel

Paris

NEUSTRIA

Mediterranean Sea

BRETONS

Loire

DUCHY OF
AQUITAINE

Dordogne

Atlantic Ocean

Bordeaux

DUCHY OF
Toulouse

Bay of
Biscay

DUCHY OF
GASCONY

UMAYYAD
CALIPHATE

Introduction: Follow the Money

Can the West make itself great again? Should it even try?

Between 1800 and the turn of this millennium, the West rose to dominate the planet. Over those two centuries, it went from being one among several peer players in an emerging global economy to producing fully eight-tenths of the world's output. Simultaneously, average incomes in the Western world, today's developed OECD economies, increased from being roughly equal to those of the rest of humanity to fifty times greater.

This overwhelming economic dominance spurred a political, cultural, linguistic and social remaking of the planet in the West's image. Almost everywhere, the nation state, a product of Europe's internal evolution, became the mainstay of political life, replacing the immense variety of city states, kingdoms, caliphates, bishoprics, sheikhdoms, chiefdoms, empires and feudal regimes that had previously dotted the globe. English became the language of global commerce, French (and later English again) that of global diplomacy. The world deposited its surpluses in Western banks, with the pound, then the dollar, replacing gold as the lubricant of trade among nations. Western universities became the meccas of aspiring intellectuals from across the world, and by the end of the twentieth century, the planet was entertaining itself with Hollywood films and European football.

Then, suddenly, history went into reverse.

As 2008's Great Recession turned into the Great Stagnation, the West's share of global output declined from 80 per cent to 60 per cent, and has continued to fall, if more slowly, since. Real wages fell, youth unemployment soared, and public services were eroded as debt – public and private – rose dramatically. Self-doubt and internal division replaced the robust self-confidence of the 1990s in Western liberal-democratic political discourse. Simultaneously, other models, particularly

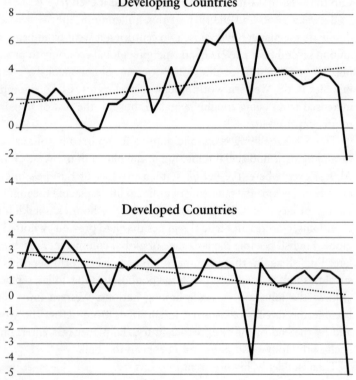

GDP Per Capita Growth (%), 1983–2020
Developing Countries

Developed Countries

Source: World Bank, World Development Indicators

the authoritarian central planning of the Chinese state, became increasingly influential on the world stage, bolstered by a Chinese economy which over the last four decades averaged an astonishing annual average growth in per capita income of over 8 per cent, which meant that actual Chinese incomes doubled every decade. Why has the balance of world power swung so dramatically against the West? Is this a decline that can be reversed, or is it a natural evolution to which the West would do better to adapt?

This is not the first time the world has witnessed such a dramatic rise and fall. Rome's rise to what was in its own terms global domination began in the second century BC, and its dominion lasted the best part of five hundred years, before crashing in the middle centuries of the first millennium AD. It may have been fifteen hundred years ago, but this book contends that Rome's demise still has important lessons for the present, using the Roman Empire, and the wider world that it spawned, to think again about the unfolding history and current situation of the contemporary West. We're not the first to think that the fate of Rome might have something to teach the modern world, but, so far, its history has been mobilized to offer a highly Western-centric diagnosis of what's going on. As the historian Niall Ferguson put it in a high-profile commentary on the Bataclan massacre in Paris in 2015, published in leading papers on either side of the Atlantic (not least the *Sunday Times* and *Boston Globe*), Europe 'has grown decadent in its shopping malls and sports stadiums' while letting in 'outsiders who have coveted its wealth without renouncing their ancestral faith . . . Like the Roman Empire in the early fifth century, Europe has *allowed* (emphasis added) its defences to crumble.' This, Ferguson concludes, 'is exactly how civilizations fall'. His inspiration here is Edward Gibbon's famous masterpiece, *Decline and Fall of the Roman Empire*, which argued that Rome suffered a slow internal erosion once it stopped resisting the outsiders – an odd mix of Christians and barbarian Goths, Vandals and others – who had begun to flourish within its borders. As if it had a virus that gradually sapped the strength of the host it penetrated, the Empire slowly decayed from its Golden Age to the point where it had effectively lost the will to live. Gibbon's basic perspective – that Rome was in charge of its own fate – remains influential today, and for some, including Ferguson, the lesson is clear. The antidote to imperial decline is to control the borders, keep out 'aliens', build walls and reaffirm the ancestral faith, while embracing more muscular nationalisms and reassessing international trade deals.[1]

But powerful as the tropes of invading barbarians and internal decadence might be, Gibbon was writing a very long time ago, his first volume published in 1776, the same year that America declared independence. And in the intervening two and a half centuries, understandings of Roman history have moved on, offering a fundamentally different perspective on the current situation the West finds itself in, and how it is likely to develop in the coming decades.

The potential for a revised Roman history to contribute to an alternative, decolonized understanding of the current position of the West became clear in a conversation between the two authors over a decade ago. Peter Heather is a Roman and post-Roman historian, with a particular interest in how living on the edge of a global Empire transformed the societies brought within its orbit. John Rapley is a political economist with a particular interest in globalization as experienced on the ground in the modern developing world. A long afternoon's discussion made it apparent that both of us were reaching similar conclusions about the unravelling of the very different empires on which we work.

Rather than having their own future entirely determined by choices and events unfolding within their own domains, we both argued that 'our' empires fundamentally began to generate the end of their own dominion because of the kind of transformations they unleashed in the world around them. Despite (and sometimes because of) the profound differences between ancient Rome and the modern West, the two histories are mutually illuminating. There is an imperial life cycle which begins with economic development. Empires come into being to generate new flows of wealth for a dominating imperial core, but, in doing so, create new wealth in both conquered provinces and some more peripheral territories too (lands and people that are not formally colonized but are drawn into subordinate economic relationships with the developing core). Such economic transformations are bound to have political consequences. Any concentration or flow of wealth is the potential building block of new political power for the actors that can harness it. As a direct result, large-scale economic development in the periphery kick-starts a political process which will eventually

challenge the domination of the imperial power that initiated the original cycle.

This economic and political logic is so powerful that some degree
of relative decline at the old imperial centre becomes inevitable. You
can't just 'make America great again' (or the UK, or the EU) because
the very exercise of Western dominance over the last few centuries has
rearranged the building blocks of global strategic power on which
that 'greatness' was based. Which also means that ill-informed attempts
directly to reverse relative decline, of the sort seen recently in 'MAGA
America' or Brexit Britain, risk only accelerating and deepening the
process. But the overall result does not have to be catastrophic civilization collapse in the form of large-scale, absolute economic decline
and widespread social, political, and even cultural dislocation.

As the history of the Roman world also emphasizes, empires can
respond to the process of adjustment with a range of possible measures, from the deeply destructive to the much more creative. The
modern West stands close to the start of its own process of adjustment; the Roman world worked fully through its own a long time
ago, and, here too, sustained comparison offers important insights.
The real significance of visible trajectories of development in the
modern West – currently at a relatively early stage – comes sharply
into focus when set alongside the longer-term changes observable as
the Roman Empire evolved and then fell apart in the half a millennium which followed the birth of Christ.

To explore the full potential of this comparison, the book is divided into two parts. Part One uses Roman history to understand the
rise of the modern West. It reveals the surprising degree to which the
internal economic and political evolution of the modern West over
the past few centuries has echoed that of the Roman Empire, and
analyses why its astonishing domination of the world economy has
ebbed so significantly and is bound to continue to do so. But where
the modern challenge from the developing periphery is still at an early
stage, the role of a rising periphery in both undermining the Roman
Empire and in generating new worlds in the aftermath of imperial
collapse can be explored in full. Therefore, Part Two takes a slightly
different approach; the two imperial narratives cannot be run side by
side since one of them is far from complete. It starts by taking a close

look at Roman collapse to identify the key factors at play in that process, while the remaining chapters examine the relevance of each of these factors to the modern West and use the ancient evidence to consider the range of longer-term outcomes – better and worse – that are today on the cards. It is not possible to make the West great again in the sense of reasserting an unchallenged global dominion, but the necessary process of adjustment can either hardwire the best of Western civilization into an emerging new global order, or undermine the best hopes for the continued prosperity of Western populations in a remade world. Ultimately, as Roman history again emphasizes, the future of the West will depend on which political and economic choices its citizens and leaders take in the pivotal years which lie ahead.

PART ONE

I

Party Like It's 399 ...

In the current political climate of bitter division and public anger over heightened inequality, stagnant living standards, rising debt and decaying public services, it's hard to remember that barely twenty years ago the future of the West looked so different. As the twentieth century entered its final year, America was the centre of the modern world. Unemployment had fallen to historic lows and the US economy – much the world's largest – was enjoying the longest burst of growth it had ever seen, the stock market rising each year by double-digits. Riding the dotcom boom, millions of Americans who owned shares grew richer by the day, spending their windfalls in a virtuous cycle that meant the economy soared. And not just America: the entire West – the rich, industrialized economies made up mostly of America's friends and allies in western Europe, Canada and Asia (Australia, New Zealand and latterly Japan) – straddled the planet like a colossus, its prosperity and values of individual liberty, democracy and free markets an unchallengeable fact of life.

Ten years earlier, in what felt like the defining historical moment of the twentieth century, East European protesters had overthrown their communist rulers. Two years after that, the Soviet Union voted itself out of existence, and American economists began jetting around the world, advising governments on the virtues of remaking their economies and political institutions in the West's image. Even China's Communist Party embraced the market. Germany reunited, Europe emerged from recession, Britannia had never been cooler, and America surged. By 1999, the share of global output consumed by the West

9

reached the highest point ever recorded: one-sixth of the planet's population consuming a staggering four-fifths of the world's output of goods and services.

In his 1999 State of the Union address, exuding an optimism that the good days would never end, US President Bill Clinton declared that 'the promise of our future is limitless'. With economists telling him that a 'Great Moderation' had taken hold, an era of economic stability which would deliver endless growth, his administration concluded that government surpluses would soon run into the trillions. As Clinton urged Congress to pour some of this vast pool of money into pensions and health care, his Treasury Secretary announced that, after decades of rising deficits, the US would finally start paying off all the debts its governments had accumulated over the previous two centuries, putting yet more money into the pockets of ordinary Americans. Meanwhile, across the Atlantic, Tony Blair's New Labour government, channelling the Zeitgeist, launched a hugely ambitious expansion of public services, all while the European Union, calmly self-confident, prepared to welcome much of the old Soviet bloc into the elite club of Western democracies.

Just a few years later, the optimism evaporated. Global financial crisis in 2008 was quickly followed by a Great Recession and then a Great Stagnation. A mere decade after its 1999 peak, the West's share of global output had shrunk by a quarter: 80 per cent of Gross Global Product had become 60 per cent. And although the worst immediate effects of the crash were quickly contained as both governments and central banks flooded their economies with money, Western countries have since failed to restore the growth rates of old, whereas growth rates in key parts of the developing world stayed high. As a result, the West's share of GGP continues to slide. And it's not just in economics that the West has been rapidly losing ground. The once-shiny Western 'brand' has lost its aura, now often presenting outsiders with an image of deeply divided indecision in democracies that increasingly seem to deliver benefits mostly to the few, restoring lost credibility to authoritarian leadership and one-party models of economic and political direction.

For some Western commentators, Gibbon's diagnosis of Rome's fall offers an obvious solution. The West is losing its identity in a tide of foreign, especially Muslim, migration; it must shore up its defences, and reaffirm core cultural values, or it is destined to tread the same path to imperial Armageddon. Roman history as it is understood in the twenty-first century, however, offers some startlingly different lessons for the modern West.

ROME, AD 399

Sixteen centuries – pretty much to the day – before Bill Clinton's Panglossian celebration of endless possibility, an imperial spokesman stood before the Senate of Rome, to give a State of the Union address for the western half of the Roman world. It was 1 January 399: inauguration day for the latest in an unbroken thousand-year line of consuls, the most prestigious office-holders of the Roman world, who were guaranteed eternal life by having the year named after them. This year's happy candidate for immortality was Flavius Manlius Theodorus, a lawyer and philosopher with a track record of administrative competence, and the speech was triumphal, heralding the dawn of a new Golden Age. After a quick flattering nod to his audience – 'It is this assembly that gives to me the measure of the universe; here I see gathered all the brilliance of the world' (a compliment that maybe not even the boldest modern spin doctor would try to pass off) – the spokesman, a poet by the name of Claudian, got down to business.

His speech had two themes. First: the brilliance of the administration which had called a man like Theodorus to office. 'Beneath such an emperor, who could refuse? Was merit ever more richly rewarded? Has any age ever produced his equal in prudence or in bravery? Even Brutus [Julius Caesar's nemesis] would be overjoyed to live under such an emperor.' Second: the prosperity that was now hardwired into the Empire. 'The path of glory lies open to the wise; merit is sure of its recognition; industry receives its due rewards.'

At first sight, the speech looks like the worst kind of self-congratulatory bullshit favoured by failing regimes throughout history. The then Western emperor Honorius was a fifteen-year-old boy, while the real ruler was a general called Stilicho: a military strongman of recent barbarian descent, surrounded by a coterie of officials who couldn't wait – literally – to sink their knives into his back.[2] Scarcely a decade later the city of Rome would be sacked by a group of barbarian warriors, recent immigrants to the Roman world, under the leadership of their own Gothic king, called Alaric. The final collapse of Honorius' realm followed within a couple of generations: the Roman West divided between a series of barbarian monarchs, with Alaric's Gothic descendants ruling much of Spain and southern Gaul, Burgundian kings in south-eastern Gaul, Frankish kings to the north, Vandals in North Africa, and a series of Anglo-Saxon warbands running wild north of the Channel. Consul, emperor, spokesman and Senate were surely all participants in a collective ceremony of wilful self-delusion? Gibbon certainly thought so. By his account, in 399, Rome had long since declined from the economic, cultural and political Golden Age of the Antonine emperors in the second century AD, and its fall was just around the corner.

Succeeding generations of historians developed Gibbon's model until, by the mid-twentieth century, a checklist of decline had been assembled which told the clearest of stories. First, there were the *agri deserti*, 'deserted fields', referred to in fourth-century imperial laws. The Empire's peasantry made up 85–90 per cent of the total population. In what was overwhelmingly an agricultural world, deserted fields clearly stank of economic disaster, to be traced back to a punitive tax regime, which was periodically complained about in contemporary writings. Second, the rot reached upwards. In Gibbon's Golden Age, the Roman middle and upper classes characteristically recorded the distinctions of their lives on dated stone inscriptions. These tablets commemorated their honours, offices and many gifts, usually of buildings and other amenities, bestowed on their local urban communities (civic virtue being highly prized in the Roman world). But thanks to two monumental nineteenth-century projects to collect and publish every known inscription in Latin and Greek, one salient, overarching point quickly became clear. In the middle of the third century AD, the annual frequency of these inscriptions suddenly collapsed to about one-fifth of its previous average. This dramatic drop-off in the self-congratulation of the wealthier classes of the Roman world, like deserted fields, smelled strongly of economic implosion. Third, close examination of Egyptian papyri and of surviving imperial coins of the same era reinforced the point. In the second half of the third century, the Empire's population had to deal with a burst of hyper-inflation not far short of the rates seen in Germany after World War I, fuelled by progressive debasements of the silver denarius. Debasement, hyper-inflation, a loss of confidence among the upper classes, and untilled fields spelled out an obvious conclusion. A century before Theodorus' inauguration, the Empire was already an economic ruin, and the rise of Christianity only added a fourth element to the chaos.

Gibbon also began a line of thought which saw the Empire's new religion as a profoundly negative development. Christian clergy and ascetics, as he saw it, amounted to thousands of 'idle mouths', whose dependence sapped the Empire's economic vitality. He also argued that Christianity's message of love – 'turn the other cheek' – undermined the martial civic virtues which had made the Roman Empire great, and he thoroughly disliked Christian leaders' propensity – in stark contrast to its founder's teachings – for arguing among themselves, which undermined the old unity of imperial purpose. As a result, the general historical consensus in the first half of the twentieth century was that, by 399, the entire Roman edifice was being held together, if barely, by a totalitarian, bloated bureaucracy sitting on top of a centralized command economy which just about managed to keep its remaining soldiers fed. The generation of scholars who came to maturity after World War I had not just observed the chaos of Weimar hyper-inflation at first hand, but were also confronted with the totalitarian examples of Bolshevik Russia and Nazi Germany. With so much going wrong in the late Empire, all that was required, according to this widely shared vision of the Roman past, was a handful of barbarian invaders, and the tattered ruin of Empire would come tumbling down: as, duly, it did, just a few decades after Theodorus' consulship supposedly inaugurated a new Golden Age.

This narrative of moral and economic rot at the imperial centre – placing responsibility for the end of Empire squarely on the shoulders of Rome's leaders – has had a contemporary impact it would be difficult to overstate. Not only popular with some leading Western conservative commentators, it can also be found in the social sciences, shaping influential strands of contemporary thought in the field of international relations. It has even wormed its way periodically into the White House. Donald Trump's former sage, Steve Bannon, regularly cited Gibbon when making his argument that America's abandonment of its religious heritage had caused decadence, a world view which found explicit mention in the new president's inaugural speech, where he characterized the current state of the country as 'American carnage'. Robert Kaplan, the writer and thinker who profoundly shaped Bill Clinton's foreign policy, also wrote glowingly of the insights he had gleaned from reading Gibbon, citing especially his influence on Kaplan's own predictions of a 'coming anarchy' in the global periphery. In economic theory, likewise, Daron Acemoglu and James Robinson argued in *Why Nations Fail* that liberal institutions set the stage for the economic triumph of the modern West, whereas autocratic ones made decline inevitable. As support for their theory, Acemoglu and Robinson cited Gibbon approvingly, arguing that Rome sealed its fate the day it ceased to be a republic, setting in motion the long but inexorable journey towards imperial collapse.

It isn't surprising that Gibbon's *Decline and Fall* should have gained particular traction in America. From the time of the Republic's birth, American intellectuals have regularly seen themselves as Rome's heirs, frequently reading its imperial history as a guide to the future of their own. An entire industry has been built on the back of different elements of Gibbon's model of internal decline. According to their own agendas, some commentators are more interested in economic failure and others in moral decay, but the emphasis is consistently on internal factors as fundamentally responsible for imperial collapse. It is a great story, beautifully told: Gibbon is still read by many for his prose alone. It also has the virtue of being old. As any teacher will tell you, the first idea that gets a firm hold in most students' brains is almost impossible to shift. But shift it must. In the last fifty years, a different Roman past has come into focus.

PLOUGHS AND POTS

In the 1950s a French archaeologist made a startling discovery in a small corner of northern Syria. What he found were the remains of some prosperous late-Roman peasants, who had spread widely across its limestone hills between the fourth and the sixth centuries AD. The natural building material in this region was its native stone, meaning that the peasants' houses, several with dating inscriptions, were still standing. Everywhere else in the Empire, peasants built in wood or mudbrick, which leave no surface traces, so this was a unique discovery. According to the standard Gibbonian model, such well-off late-Roman peasants should not have been there. Wasn't over-taxation driving them out of business, their fields bare, leaving no space for this kind of rural prosperity?

In the same decade, cultural historians were also beginning to explore some avenues which undermined much of Gibbon's charge sheet against the Christian religion. Some of it had never been more than a sly joke. Given the overall history of Christianity as an organized religion from Emperor Constantine onwards – encompassing crusades, inquisition and forced conversions – the idea that it might ever have undermined Roman imperialism by encouraging too much pacifism was Gibbon's wicked sense of humour at play. More detailed and balanced investigation since the 1950s has also made it clear that Christianity did not so much undermine classical cultural unity as lead it in exciting new directions. Christianity, as it evolved in the fourth and fifth centuries, was a vigorous, innovative synthesis of Biblical and classical cultural elements, and the problems posed by religious division have been massively overstated. In both practice and theory, emperors quickly came to function as head of a Church structure, which did a pretty good job of fostering a new type of cultural unity across the vast expanse of imperial rule. Nor does the 'idle mouths' argument, in relation to the Christian clergy, carry much conviction. Senior Christian posts quickly came to be occupied by the provincial Roman gentry, who both led Church services and upheld the existing social and political order, while, in a general sense, being neither more nor less 'idle' than the elite Roman landowning class had ever been. In practice, clergy of all kinds largely operated as state functionaries, not subversive representatives of a hostile culture.

The image of late-Roman government as a failing authoritarian state has been similarly undermined in the face of new scholarship. In 1964 a former wartime British civil servant turned professor of ancient history – A. H. M. Jones – published an exhaustive analysis of the Roman Empire's operations, which blew substantial holes in the old orthodoxy. The imperial bureaucracy did expand in the fourth century, but, in comparative terms, remained far too small to exercise tight control over the vast expanse of the Roman world, which on its longest diagonal stretched from Scotland to Iraq. Nor, in fact, was the imperial centre in charge of the process. As we'll see in Chapter 2, it was provincial Roman elites themselves who drove forward bureaucratic expansion by demanding new positions within its structures. What at first sight looks like authoritarian governmental expansion is actually the Empire's existing ruling classes relocating their traditional struggles for favour and influence to a new socio-political context. A not insignificant development, certainly, but not something heralding the end of the imperial system in any obvious way. All of these were substantial revisions to the old paradigm of Roman decline, but they remained isolated glimpses of an alternative Roman history. In the 1970s a revolutionary new discovery then brought these individual observations together into a fundamental paradigm shift – one which bears striking testimony to the ubiquity of human clumsiness.

Broken pottery has two key features. Once broken, it is more or less useless. But the individual shards themselves endure. As a result, shattered crockery tends to stay where it was dropped, giving us a map of the houses and villages of its original owners long after wood has rotted and mudbrick returned to dust. Two technical breakthroughs were required, however, before human cack-handedness could fully unlock the macro-history of Roman economic development. First, the shards had to be dated. Designs of Roman dinner services ('fine wares' in archaeologists' jargon) and of storage jars (*amphorae*) had long been known to change over time, but researchers had to find enough of them in sites that could be dated to build up a chronologically accurate picture of their evolving designs. Second, they had to be able to recognize what density of surface pottery indicated that an ancient settlement lay hidden beneath the ground. By the 1970s both problems had been solved, thanks to modern ploughing, which bites deep enough into the subsoil to bring long-buried materials back to the surface.

What followed shows that real archaeology is usually much less

fun than Indiana Jones. Over the next twenty years, small armies of
students and teachers lined up across the former Roman landscape to
pick up every piece of broken pottery they could find within a one-
metre square placed directly in front of them. Everything was put in
labelled plastic bags. The line then advanced a metre, and repeated
the process. And again, and again, until it had covered the entirety of
its target region, or until the season ended. Winters were spent analys-
ing the contents of the bags. Not surprisingly, large-scale rural surveys
could take a decade and more to complete. But archaeologists are
nothing if not patient, and the 1970s and 1980s were full of them,
bags in hand, surveying wide tracts of the old Roman world.

The process may have been dull, but the results were spectacular.
The Roman Empire was an immense place. It looks huge on the map,
but you have to factor in, too, that everything in antiquity moved
about twenty times less fast – at least overland: by foot, in carts, or on
horseback – than now. The real measure of distance is how long it
takes an actual person to get from A to B, not some arbitrary unit of
measurement, so that the different localities of the Roman Empire
were twenty times further apart in practice than they appear to the
naked modern eye, and the whole Empire was actually twenty times
as vast. But for all this extraordinary size, when the results came in,
rural settlement more or less everywhere in the Roman world, and
not just in the limestone hills of northern Syria, turned out to have
been at its peak in the fourth century, right on the eve of its political
collapse. Southern Britain, northern and southern Gaul, Spain, North
Africa, Greece, Turkey, and the Middle East: contrary to expectation,
all produced similar results. Rural population densities, and consequently overall agricultural output, reached maximum levels in the
late-imperial period. And since Rome's was overwhelmingly an agricultural economy, there's not the slightest doubt that Gross Imperial
Product – the total economic output of the Roman world – reached
higher peaks in the fourth century than at any previous point in the
entirety of Roman history.

This is a staggering discovery. A massive and ever-expanding
dataset – the number of pottery shards buried in the earth is beyond
number – has demonstrated that the trajectory of Roman macro-
economic development was exactly the opposite of what the narrative

of decline had supposed. As a result, this unshakeable accumulated tonnage of new evidence has necessarily forced a rethink of the much more limited checklist on which the old orthodoxy had been based.

Agri deserti, on closer inspection, turns out to be a technical term for land that was not productive enough to be worth taxing. Crucially, it carried no necessary implication that the fields in question had *ever* been farmed. The end of stone inscriptions is a more important historical phenomenon, but again, on further reflection, no clear measure of economic decline. Up to the mid-third century, the empire's local upper classes spent their time competing for dominance in their home towns, where they had sizeable council budgets to spend. The gift-giving recorded in these inscriptions was a key weapon in that political competition. But in the century's mid-point the imperial centre confiscated those budgets (for reasons we'll return to), and the whole reason for local political competition disappeared. The new game in town for ambitious provincial landowners then became joining a rapidly expanding imperial bureaucracy, which now controlled the purse strings. Provincial landowners refashioned their lives accordingly, with expensive legal education – as per our lawyer turned consul of 399, Theodorus – replacing local generosity as the path to success. In this new environment, there was much less incentive to record your generosity via the commissioning of an expensive inscription. As for taxation, one basic point to remember is that intensive comparative historical investigation has never yet managed to identify a human society which considered itself insufficiently taxed. Late Roman taxpayers' complaints are not particularly sustained, and the new archaeological evidence for rural prosperity makes it clear that they could not have been suffering under too punitive a fiscal regime. The hyper-inflation was real enough, but its impact was more limited than previously thought. What was inflated was the price (of absolutely everything) as measured in debased silver coins. But the bulk of the wealth of Roman landowners was held in the form of reserves of pure precious metals, and above all in their actual land and its produce. None of this was affected by progressive silver currency debasements, so that, unlike Weimar Germany, Roman hyper-inflation left the real wealth of imperial landowning elites untouched.

What used to be taken as clear evidence of economic decline, isn't. Gibbon was wrong. The Roman Empire did not endure a long, slow decay from its second-century Golden Age, until its fall became inevitable in the fifth.[3] Imperial prosperity peaked right on the eve of collapse. The spokesman of AD 399, while certainly serving the interests both of himself and the regime that employed him, was neither stupid nor criminally duplicitous in proclaiming a new Golden Age. At the end of the fourth century, the famous *Pax Romana* – the era of broad political and legal stability created by the conquests of the legions – had endured for the best part of half a millennium, creating the macro-economic conditions which allowed the provinces of the Empire to increase in prosperity for centuries.

This revolution in understandings of the later Roman Empire has some potentially momentous implications, if we consider the striking contrast between the extravagant Western triumphalism of the 1990s and the current atmosphere of doom and gloom. The first lesson from Roman history is clear: imperial collapse doesn't have to be preceded by long-term economic decline. The Roman Empire was the largest and longest-lived state western Eurasia has ever known, but half of it crumbled into non-existence within a few decades of its economic peak. By itself, this could be a random coincidence. Deeper exploration of the longer-term histories of Rome and the modern West suggests, however, that it is anything but.

2

Empire and Enrichment

In 371 a Christian poet called Decimius Magnus Ausonius from what is now Bordeaux devoted 483 Latin hexameters to proclaiming the glories of one particular north-western corner of the Roman world: the valley of the river Moselle, in present-day Germany, which eventually flows into the Rhine. What attracted his eye was the region's well-tended agricultural riches and the human culture that had grown around it:

> The roofs of country-houses, perched high on the overhanging river banks, the hillsides green with vines, and the pleasant stream of the Moselle gliding below with subdued murmuring.

As he warmed to his theme, Ausonius dwelt at length on the many delicious fish of the river (their names a great opportunity for him to show off his mastery of Latin metre), the simple pleasures of peasant life, and the grandeur of the region's manor houses:

> Who has the skill to unfold the countless embellishments and forms, and to display the architectural beauties of each demesne?

The *Mosella* belongs to an old Latin literary genre – the *ekphrasis* or extended description – but has a radical subtext. Ausonius' point is that the Roman life along the river's banks is so rich that even the Tiber (used as a metaphor for the city of Rome) 'would not dare to set his glories above thine'. In the end, Ausonius playfully withdraws the point, lest he be accused of hubris, but the rest of the poem leaves the audience in no doubt where the poet's real feelings lie. And while we might be tempted to dismiss Ausonius' claim as poetic licence run wild, it actually strikes a chord with the most remarkable anomaly to emerge from the broken pottery shards.

MOVEABLE WEALTH

Although the Empire as a whole was enjoying a golden fourth century – including Ausonius' precious Moselle valley, which was indeed home to many rich late-Roman villas – the pottery surveys did identify some specific areas of decline. Two are easily explained. Rural settlement in northern Britain and Belgium had never recovered from some intense barbarian raiding which had affected these areas in the third century (more on this later). Much more puzzling, however, are the results from the Empire's Italian heartlands. Italy did not suffer anywhere near as heavily in the third century, but settlement and agricultural output there peaked in the two hundred years either side of the birth of Christ, before declining to steady but significantly lower levels in the third and fourth centuries AD. Why did the original imperial centre contract, when the farthest reaches of its Empire were booming? The solution begins to emerge if we fast-forward a thousand years and analyse the rise of what would eventually become the modern West.

At the start of the second millennium AD, what would become the modern West was anything but an economic powerhouse. A couple of Vikings had made it across the Atlantic, but at that point North America played no meaningful part in broader European economic and political networks. Muslim armies from North Africa and the Middle East ruled southern Spain and had reduced Constantinople to a small rump successor state, depriving it of the vast majority of its possessions in the southern and eastern Mediterranean hinterland. Squeezed in between was a poor, technologically backward, politically fragmented, and disease-ridden corner of the globe. Yet over the next millennium this rustic little region would rise to dominate the planet.

What initiated such a dramatic turnaround remains hotly contested. Political factors had something to do with it. European states were neither too powerful nor too weak, so that entrepreneurs enjoyed both the freedom and stability they needed to undertake risky ventures. The natural environment helped too. Europe possessed an abundance of domesticable animal species (an early form of capital), lots of waterways for cheap navigation, and a varied landscape that produced a wide range of crops, all of which encouraged and facilitated exchange. Culture may have also played a role. In the eyes of some analysts, Western Christianity's stress on consensual marriage produced nuclear families, which had incentives for saving, while its universalist morality and trust-based economy facilitated contracts with strangers, materially assisting long-distance trade. For others, the emergence of a fully developed legal concept of private property, the product of Europe's medieval universities (drawing on Roman precedent), was central to the process.

There is little disagreement, however, about what happened next. Technological advances in the Middle Ages, such as the adoption of heavy enough ploughs to get the best out of clay soils and more sophisticated crop-rotation schemes, generated bigger agricultural surpluses. This led to an increase in luxury consumption among European elites, their taste for Eastern sugar, spices and silk clothing further stirred by the experience of crusade. In return, Europe's developing economy began producing more refined woollen cloths, which found a ready market in the East. This growing long-distance trade in turn sustained a thickening network of markets and fairs.

The earliest and most significant of these were in central and northern Italy, where geography – particularly easy access to the Mediterranean for longer-distance trade – conspired with the relative weakness of landowning elites to make merchants rich enough to dominate political agendas in their local communities. The resulting city states built the social, political and legal infrastructure which helped trade expand still further: credit and financial markets, contract-enforcing mechanisms, secure sea lanes and foreign trade agreements. Sitting at the crossroads of Europe and the Orient, Italian merchants largely controlled the exchange of European exports (especially in cloth and wheat) for Eastern goods. From the eleventh century onwards, these Italian city states, with Florence, Venice, and Genoa at their head, rose to dominate European trade.

But the prosperity of this initial Italian core quickly prompted development elsewhere. Although the Italian city states sold European cloth to the East, the best products came from the Low Countries, which in turn imported much of their raw wool from England. On the back of the Italian trade networks, therefore, north European economies began to expand and diversify. Some northern cities, particularly in Flanders, where textile factories had appeared as early as the twelfth and thirteenth centuries, began to rival their Italian counterparts as centres of trade and commerce from the later 1400s and 1500s. More generally, the huge profits earned by the Italian city states from the Eastern trade then prodded other European governments to get in on the action. Rather than contest Italian dominance of the Eastern Mediterranean, Atlantic states chose to go west to find an alternative sea route to Asia. Led by the Portuguese and Spanish, Europeans improved their navigational and ship-building technologies to the point that they could take to the high seas. Bumping accidentally into the Americas en route, they didn't anticipate how these (to them) new lands would transform Europe itself, and for many decades European trade remained centred on the east, via the Mediterranean. Over the longer term, however, as American gold and silver began to swell the treasuries of Spain and Portugal, and north European merchants opened up new sea routes to the east, the focus of European capitalism shifted away from Italy and towards its outer edges.

Swollen with American riches, however, the Spanish and Portuguese empires tended to import luxury manufactured goods from the existing European industrial regions, and to bank their surpluses elsewhere (notably Germany), rather than transforming their own economies. This prompted further expansion in the north. In particular, the demand for English textiles eventually spawned a dramatic economic revolution north of the Channel, not least because the English Parliament had the power to alter the rules of land tenure. Estate owners with an eye on new opportunities petitioned to enclose their lands, evicting the peasantry to raise sheep for a burgeoning textile industry. As the landowners grew rich, creating new sources of capital for investment, the enclosures also created a generation of landless labourers desperate for work, offering the growing industrial sector an abundant supply of cheap labour at an earlier date than in any of Britain's rivals. By the late eighteenth century, craft workshops had spread across the British countryside to take advantage of this changed environment. At the same time the Dutch and British, along with the French, had caught up with – and overtaken – the Iberian states in building fleets that could seize assets overseas.

With the growth of its manufacturing sector generating an insatiable appetite for raw materials, Britain aggressively exploited its colonial holdings, the most important of which quickly came to be in North America. And even though the United States eventually broke away from Britain politically, it continued to play a key role as both supplier and market for British industrial goods, its cotton eventually becoming even more important to Britain's growing cloth industry than India's. By the nineteenth century, this industry had substantially relocated to Britain's cities, where plentiful labour enabled business owners to run much larger factories, with armies of labourers working the new machinery that was then being invented at such a rapid pace. And, as the nineteenth century wore on, the US joined Britain's other European rivals, France and Germany above all, in using government policy to nurture the development of its own manufacturing industries, rather than leaving it to the free market as Britain had done.

By the end of the century, most of Britain's population already lived in cities, compared to only about a quarter in France. At that point, however, Britain was already being leap-frogged by its former American subjects who, having dispossessed the land's indigenous occupants, were opening up vast western territories for settlement. Hence the United States welcomed massive immigration throughout the nineteenth and early twentieth centuries, doubling its population every few years: a rate of expansion no European rival could match. Not only did this lead to huge increases in output, but it also generated massive new markets for the country's growing industrial sector. In the face of large-scale exploitation and resulting protests, wages eventually began to rise. But while America saw the same sort of rioting and socialist agitation that spread through European cities at this time, the country had an important release valve which kept a lid on labour costs. Malcontents could try their luck out west, and new workers could always be found to replace them at the gates of Ellis Island, the point of entry to the United States. As a result of this relentless growth, the US had surpassed Britain in total economic output by the end of the nineteenth century, entering its Gilded Age.

The millennium of economic evolution in the western hemisphere was thus punctuated by periodic shifts in the geographical epicentre of maximum prosperity. The growth of capitalism drove forward an unceasing demand for new markets, new products, and new sources of supply, which steadily pushed its location outwards from its original north Italian heartland. A straightforward logic – based on the availability of labour and raw materials – dictated startling overall levels of economic growth across the whole of the emerging West in the later medieval and modern eras. First northern Italy, then Spain and Portugal, Holland, France and Britain in turn, and finally the United States rose to economic dominance as new opportunities interacted with the emergence of new sources of raw materials and labour, to allow each in turn to dominate valuable export trades. At each transition, even as improved transportation facilitated the emergence of new trade networks, the bulk of local production was consumed locally or at most regionally.[4] Nonetheless, the crucial variable which really shifted the epicentre of prosperity was the extra wealth created by export trades in the different eras.

If we return to Rome, the rise of the modern West helps explain the initially mysterious decline of the Empire's original Italian heartlands. Here, too, straightforward economic logic dictated a shift in economic dominance away from an original imperial centre. In this case, industrial production played almost no role in the changing patterns of prosperity within the borders of the Empire, whose economy remained overwhelmingly agricultural in nature. In the first centuries BC and AD, Italian-based wine and olive oil industries – plus to some extent pottery too, and possibly grain, although that is archaeologically invisible – exported their products in large quantities, particularly to Rome's newly acquired European possessions. Over time, the agricultural resources of the rest of the Empire, in the macro-economic conditions created by the *Pax Romana*, were developed much more fully and entirely eclipsed this early Italian dominance, not least because transportation technology was so limited and expensive.

With carts moving at a maximum twenty-five miles a day, it could take weeks to move goods between the Empire's provinces overland: a far cry from the trains and ships that would weave together modern empires. Not only that, but the price of a wagon of wheat, as reported in Diocletian's *Prices Edict* from AD 300, doubled for every fifty miles travelled: an increase driven by the need both to feed the oxen and to pay a plethora of internal tolls. In this context, as conquered lands began their own intensive production, local and therefore inherently cheaper products were bound to drive out Italian imports.

By the later imperial period, long-distance trade prevailed only if an item could not physically be produced locally (wine and olive oil, for instance, in non-Mediterranean landscapes), or if it commanded a particularly high price premium (rare types of marble or expensive vintages, compared to common or garden local varieties). The other exception was where goods could piggyback on transport structures that the state was subsidizing for its own purposes, primarily to feed the great imperial capitals or for military supply (the shipowners who moved grain, wine and oil across the Mediterranean at the state's behest seem to have moonlighted by carrying other goods in their holds). But these interventions were few, and the logic of transport costs had long since driven forward Roman provincial development at the expense of the old Italian heartland. The bloated city of Rome itself had become a vast importer of wine, oil and other necessities from Spain, North Africa and the broader Mediterranean.[5]

PROVINCIALS

Behind these macro-economic shifts, and powering them forward, lay millions of individual histories. Ausonius' was one of them. He wasn't himself from the Moselle valley, an undertone of local Gallic pride creeping into the start of his poem:

> The whole gracious prospect [of the Moselle valley] made me behold a picture of my own native land, the gracious and well-tended country of Bordeaux. [ll. 18–19]

The deepest roots of his family are lost to us, but they belonged to the tribe of the Bitigures Vivisci who had originally been subdued by Julius Caesar, four centuries before Ausonius came to Trier in the Moselle valley. Once the Celtic hill fort of Burgidala, Bordeaux was refounded post-conquest as a Roman city with a council drawn from the local tribal nobility, who eventually acquired all the necessary trappings of imperial culture – learning Latin, building villas, baths and temples – and used local office-holding as a path to Roman citizenship. Ausonius' father emerged from this background to become a prominent university teacher in the new eastern imperial capital of Constantinople. Ausonius himself graduated from university teaching to private tutor for the reigning emperor's son, and, on the latter's succession, held some of the highest offices of state, including eventually the consulship itself.

This story of family success, over two generations, unfolded from a base of solid, developing agricultural prosperity. The Bordeaux region was already a centre of wine production in the Roman period, growing wealthier thanks to the political and economic stability afforded by the *Pax Romana*. The family combined this with intense engagement with the cultural requirements of participation in Roman public life, and a sharp eye for the best route to even greater prosperity. By the fourth century, serving on your town council was no longer such an attractive option because, as we saw in the first chapter, the Empire had confiscated the revenues which the councils used to control. Much better, as with Ausonius père et fils, to engage with the developing imperial system where all the money and influence now lay. Many of Ausonius' peers demanded and received jobs at various levels in the expanding imperial bureaucracy, others became lawyers like Theodorus, while the Ausonii trod a well-established path via cultural distinction to worldly success. As far as the Roman elite was concerned, its shared, distinctive culture – based on the intensive study of language and literature – was what made it a uniquely civilized and rational society, so learning was a powerful card in the game of self-advancement.[6] But in every case the profits acquired through engaging with the structures of Empire were ploughed back into expanded portfolios of landed estates back home. Ausonius' academic-cum-political career at court was no exception. When push came to shove, land was the only solid investment in Rome's overwhelmingly agricultural economy.

A similar collection of individual success stories drove forward the evolution of the modern Western Empire. Like those of the ancient Ausonii, the origins of the great Vanderbilt family are obscure. In the seventeenth century, when European trading companies were avidly acquiring overseas colonies, the Dutch West Indies company was chartered in the Netherlands. One of its first ventures was to establish a trading post on the southern tip of Manhattan Island, which became the capital of New Amsterdam. To provision the fort, farmers were imported from Holland, who quickly discovered that the soil was richer on the long island to the east of Manhattan: Breuckelen (later anglicized as Brooklyn).

One of these farmers was Jan Aertsen ('son of Aert'). Because he came from the Utrecht village of Bilt, he also went by Vanderbilt ('from Bilt'). A penniless thirteen-year-old at the time of his emigration in 1640, he was indentured to a Dutch settler for three years, after which he set up his own farm. From 1661 his name begins to appear in the written records, and by the end of the century the family was well-established on Long Island. By this time the British had taken over the colony and renamed it New York, but the Vanderbilts joined many Dutch settlers in happily adapting to the new regime. They learned English to interact with the new government and a growing number of British colonists, but otherwise life continued much as before. In the later eighteenth century, most Dutch families were still conducting the bulk of their business and social affairs in their native tongue.

Flexible and pragmatic, they readily adjusted to another new regime when the United States declared themselves independent in 1776. As the new nation grew ever more prosperous, trade expanded, and the first Cornelius Vanderbilt, Jan's great-great-great-grandson, who was twelve in 1776, started supplementing his farming income with a small boat that carried produce to the city. His namesake-son, born in 1794, ultimately abandoned farming altogether and, with a bit of family money, bought himself a slightly larger boat to ferry goods and people to and from the city. So successful was this venture that he quickly acquired more boats, and when war broke out again between Britain and America in 1812, still more were needed to provision America's coastal ports. Expanding afterwards into steam, and then to trans-Atlantic liners, the 'Commodore' finally diversified into railways in the mid-nineteenth century, prospering mightily when the federal government opened up the West to European settlement. As the prairies poured mountains of grain on to European markets, and millions of Europeans flooded in to farm, Vanderbilt's sea and railway empires exploded.

In several important ways the two family histories bear little resemblance to one another. Ausonius managed to climb the social ladder at a time of relative economic and technological stasis. Patterns of productivity within the Roman system changed little from one year to the next, so the opportunities for advancement were limited: make an initial fortune from wine and other agricultural products, use it to acquire the necessary cultural capital to prosper further in the social and political networks of Empire, then plough the profits back into an expanded portfolio of landed estates. The Vanderbilts, on the other hand, particularly the two Cornelii, lived through one of the most dramatic periods of technological and economic revolution ever known, so the family could exploit entirely new possibilities as trade and production changed around them. But in another, more fundamental respect, the two histories actually repeat the same basic pattern: ambitious provincial clans seizing the opportunities of Empire to transform the trajectories of their family histories.

In their different contexts, if not always with the same colossal degree of success, the histories of the Vanderbilts and Ausonii were replicated a million times over as the arcs of their respective imperial histories unfolded. From Britain to Syria, thousands of members of (usually) existing pre-Roman local elites maximized their position to become proper and prosperous imperial citizens, with a healthy dose of Roman legionary veterans and minor Italian administrators thrown into the burgeoning mix of provincial society. It was, of course, steadily the increasing prosperity of these families which powered the economic rise of what were originally outlying areas and the relative eclipse of the old Italian heartlands of Empire. The boundaries of the Roman Empire formed where the legions came to a halt, and within that frontier arc a mix of immigrants and Romanized natives built up the agricultural prosperity which supported the imperial edifice.

The modern Western Empire, likewise, was created by the conquerors and settlers who exploited the new opportunities opened up by recently acquired land, labour, and natural resources. The scale of the modern migration was incomparably vast compared to anything generated by the workings of Roman imperialism. At its peak, in the decades straddling the turn of the twentieth century, some 55 million Europeans left for the 'New World'. Push met pull in this process. The pull came from the lands being prised open by European empires, the push from within Europe itself, where a surge in the labour supply combined with technological change was forcing people off the land.

Advances in medical technology, particularly the spread of vaccination and improvements in public sanitation, led to astonishing rises in Western life expectancy, especially from about 1870 when child mortality levels began to dip dramatically (see p. 31). In Germany, infant death rates stood at 50 per cent in the mid-nineteenth century, before spiralling rapidly downwards in subsequent decades, as did those in other European countries from a slightly lower but still horrifying starting point of around 30 per cent. But while more children were surviving, average family sizes took several generations to adjust downwards. As a result, an extraordinary moment in demographic history saw Europeans increase massively as a proportion of the total population of the globe. From a historic level of about 15 per cent population share – roughly the level to which it has since retreated – by the time of World War I one in four people on the planet were Europeans. In the same era, improving agricultural technology, which permitted more intensive cultivation of the land, also drastically cut the need for farm labour. Moreover, where traditional agricultural patterns persisted alongside the new larger farms, as in southern Europe, average farm sizes grew steadily smaller as the land was subdivided further with each passing generation. The result was that even those who remained on the land could not live off it. The attraction of the colonies became irresistible for many.

In what were at that point relative economic backwaters, now-independent governments in countries like the United States and Canada, eager to accelerate development, did not restrict their appeals to the old heartlands of Empire, instead reaching out to any European regions with abundant supplies of labour, especially southern and eastern Europe. Some of these immigrants, like the Oppenheimers, Carnegies, Rockefellers and Bronfmans, followed the Vanderbilts, starting out as poor settlers to build vast fortunes. The overall effect, by the end of the nineteenth century, was that the world's richest families were no longer European royals or British industrialists, but new tycoons who had made their fortunes across the Atlantic. And like the Ausonii in antiquity, the grandest of these new families often cemented their rise by returning in triumph to the old imperial centre, marrying into European noble families (as the Vanderbilts did) to acquire the class distinction to complement their wealth. Given that Europe's aristocracies, their wealth based largely on agriculture, were then often facing at least relative economic decline, this arrangement suited both sides.

Most migrants did not acquire wealth and social status on anything like such a scale, and many others played a completely involuntary part in the process. Between the sixteenth and the nineteenth centuries, the Atlantic slave trade forced an estimated 12 million Africans onto ships to be transported to plantations in the Americas to cultivate sugar and cotton. Unknown numbers died long before they got there.

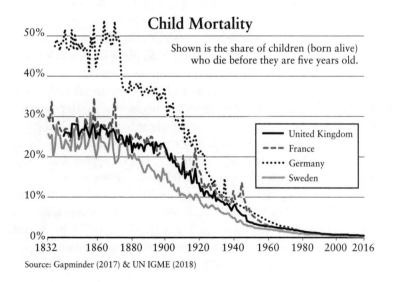

Child Mortality

Shown is the share of children (born alive) who die before they are five years old.

United Kingdom
France
Germany
Sweden

Source: Gapminder (2017) & UN IGME (2018)

This horrific and long-term movement of people altered the economic trajectory of the Americas in ways that would transform the world. But whether they had migrated voluntarily or been forced to do so, it was these great masses of humanity on the move which meant that the former provincial fringes of the Empire finally surpassed its original heartlands in prosperity. These individual family histories provide a deeper understanding of why the epicentres of imperial prosperity should have shifted over the centuries, and a further dimension of Ausonius' *Mosella* brings the underlying process fully into focus.

TWO WESTERN EMPIRES

It's highly unusual to have any evidence for the immediate reception of an ancient work of literature, but the *Mosella* provides a fascinating exception. It provoked an instant letter of complaint from a blue-blooded Roman senator called Quintus Aurelius Symmachus. The problem: Ausonius hadn't sent him his own copy. Symmachus said he admired the work, though he did poke some fun – gentle or otherwise – at all the fish Ausonius mentioned. ('And yet, although I have often found myself at your table and marvelled at most other articles of food . . . I have never found there fish such as you describe.') But the senator had been forced to peek at someone else's copy doing the rounds in Rome. When you dig a bit deeper, it becomes clear that his omission from the distribution list was no oversight.

Two years before, Symmachus had led a senatorial embassy to the city of Trier in the Moselle valley, where the western court of Valentinian I was then based. Trier is where Symmachus had got to know Ausonius and dined with him – perhaps underwhelmed by his fish course. During this embassy he gave several speeches at Valentinian's court, which survive only in fragments. Even so, one of them is highly revealing. Symmachus' take on Rome's north-west frontier was strikingly different from Ausonius' *Mosella*. Symmachus did not concentrate on the profoundly Roman character of the region, but on the heroic role played by the 'semi-barbaric Rhine' in protecting the Tiber (read 'Rome'): the centre of imperial civilization.

Which suddenly brings out the real significance of Ausonius' poem: the *Mosella* was a proud Gallic provincial's answer to the patronizing attitude of the Roman grandee. As you might expect, Ausonius' version went down infinitely better than Symmachus' speeches at court in Trier. Symmachus was sent home from the embassy with the dismissive dignity of 'count third class' (as bad as it sounds, and with the added fun that it was an act of treason not to use an imperial dignity that you had been granted, so Symmachus was forced to advertise his lack of success forever more), while Ausonius graduated from imperial tutor to high offices of state in the mid-370s, and eventually to the consulship itself in 379. This entertainingly fraught exchange between Ausonius and Symmachus points us towards another key insight generated by a comparison of Rome and the modern West: the question of political development.

The Roman Empire started life, as empires do, as a conquest state. Most of the provinces brought under Rome's formal dominion at sword point witnessed not just the initial brutalities of subjugation, but at least one major revolt afterwards. Boudicca's whirlwind destruction of Colchester, St Albans, London and part of the ninth legion in AD 60 was pretty much par for the course. But these revolts usually occurred during the first few decades of Roman rule, and, over time, the political status of the provinces and of elite provincials like the Ausonii changed out of all recognition. The economic dominance of the formerly conquered provinces was matched – as the spat between Ausonius and Symmachus illustrates – by a fundamental political transformation. From the second century AD onwards, the Empire remained a nominally united entity run from Rome, but given its vast scale and rudimentary communications, the capital city's command over outlying regions became increasingly limited. By the late imperial period, what held the imperial edifice together was not a domineering centre, but something much more powerful: common financial and legal structures, sitting on top of deeply held cultural values shared right across a now much more broadly defined ruling Roman class of provincial landowners.

By 399, after four hundred years of Empire, Rome's former conquered subjects had long since adapted to the brave new world first carved out by the legions. If you wanted to get anywhere within this colossal structure in the early period, you had first to acquire Roman citizenship and join the imperial cult, both of which required provincial elites to recreate their own decent approximations of high imperial culture. By the fourth century, as Ausonius' career shows us, the most profitable career paths lay in imperial service, and as such the vast expansion of the bureaucracy was the product of provincial consumer demand, not totalitarian bureaucratic design. Throughout, success required provincial elites to buy absolutely (and expensively) into the Empire's Greco-Roman cultural norms, with the result, by the fourth century, that provincials from Hadrian's Wall to the Euphrates had wholeheartedly adopted their conquerors' Latin, towns, togas and philosophy of life. Even Christianity spread by virtue of its incorporation into the culture of the governing class, and, as the spat between Ausonius and Symmachus makes clear, a provincial official from Bordeaux could now use Latin literature to teach a blue-blooded senator a sharp – if civil – lesson.

The original conquest state run from Rome had evolved into a vast, western Eurasian commonwealth, with a common taxation structure that was used to maintain the army. The army, in turn, protected the imperial edifice, a legal structure which defined and preserved the provincial elites' prosperity and the shared sense of their own moral and ethical superiority that had been drummed into them by their education. The Empire was not even run from Rome anymore, because it was too far away from the key frontiers: on the Rhine and Danube in Europe, and the Euphrates looking towards Persia. This was the era of the 'inside-out empire', run from new political and economic centres much closer to the frontier. Even when, for practical reasons, it proved necessary to divide the Empire politically, with an eastern half run from Constantinople, and its western counterpart from Trier on the Rhine or Milan in northern Italy, the legal and cultural unity of the Empire survived. When Theodorus received his consulship, Rome was a great educational, cultural and symbolic centre, but that was all: 'a sacred precinct', as one fourth-century commentator put it, 'far from the highway'.

Lesson two from Roman imperial history is prosaic but profound. Empires are not static entities, 'things'. They are dynamic systems of economic and political integration. Any long-lived empire will therefore evolve over time as different elements of the system change in relationship to one another, and transform the overall structures of the system itself. Consequently, major changes in the location of economic power will quickly be matched by corresponding transformations in political influence.

This provides us with a lens through which to view the evolution of the modern Western Empire. Even those who might deny its whole existence – on the reasonable grounds that we're not dealing with a single entity established by a series of conquests or organized from one metropolitan centre – cannot deny the overall continuity in the growth of the Western economy, which culminated in its extraordinary share of global GDP by the year 1999. At that point, despite its sometimes violently competitive origins – the first truly global conflict in the history of humankind was fought out between Britain and France in a series of wars over the eighteenth century – the globally dominant position of the Western bloc of nations was built upon deep levels of internal economic integration in terms of trade, capital flows, and human migration. Huge numbers of immigrants from the old European centres of empire helped create their successor – the modern United States – making it unsurprising that there also are important shared ties and values, manifest in the inter-marriage of American with European elites, and American mimicking of the models of European culture. When Vanderbilt transplanted that pinnacle of European high culture, a university, to the United States, endowing a college that would eventually bear his name, its applicants were expected to work fluently in Latin and Greek.

Eventually, this common culture of empire, the modern equivalent to Latin, towns and togas, found formal legal, financial, and institutional expression: a modern counterpart to the rise of the provinces to economic and political dominance within the inside-out Roman imperial system of the fourth century. After World War II, when the United States enjoyed a period of hegemony so complete it could discipline its squabbling allies, it led the creation of a series of institutions – the United Nations, the World Bank and International Monetary Fund, NATO, the General Agreement on Tariffs and Trade, the OECD, the G7 – which enshrined the global dominance of Western governments – and the principles they espoused: markets, liberty, democracy, national sovereignty, and the multilateral order. Agreeing to disagree on the details of their respective national models (particularly over the provision of government services and foreign policy), the countries of the West united around a set of shared values that enabled a high degree of cooperation in their relations. Overseeing it all, as in ancient Rome, was a dominant military power, the United States, able to ensure a measure of continuity and stability in the furthest outreaches of empire.

Understood properly as durable, evolving imperial systems, the political evolution of these two Western empires is not as different as initial appearances might suggest. The Roman Empire was created by conquest, but evolved into a globally dominant (in its own context) commonwealth resting on a bedrock of shared financial, cultural and legal structures. Its modern counterpart emerged from intense internal conflict among its eventual partners, but, by 1999, had ended up in much the same place: a self-identifying body with important common values operating through a common set of legal and financial institutions.

Two strong parallels between the histories of Rome and the modern West have emerged. Crisis hit both systems at their points of apparent maximum prosperity, and, over the long term, both had seen periodic shifts in the internal epicentres of economic and political dominance. These parallels are anything but accidental. The reason why crisis should hit deeply entrenched imperial systems at their points of maximum prosperity emerges with clarity when we turn our attention outwards, because imperial systems don't cease to operate at the limits of their formal frontiers. In their ascendancy, both empires grew rich off the world around them. But in doing so, they inadvertently transformed the geo-strategic context in which they were operating, and in this lay the roots of their own demise.

3

East of the Rhine, North of the Danube

Round about the year AD 30 a Roman merchant called Gargilius Secundus purchased a cow from a man called Stelos. Stelos came from beyond the frontier – the kind of person Romans dismissed as barbarians, regarding them as inferior by definition – living near the modern Dutch town of Franeker, east of the Rhine. The transaction cost 115 silver *nummi*; we know about it because a record was inscribed on a piece of wood which was dredged out of a Dutch river. A small-scale and entirely unremarkable exchange: if it happened once on Rome's European frontiers, it happened a million times. In the centuries either side of the birth of Christ, huge numbers of Roman soldiers were stationed on the Rhine frontier: a vast, unprecedented source of economic demand; 22,000 Roman soldiers, for instance, were established on the territory of probably only about 14,000 recently subdued, indigenous occupants (known as Cananifates) of its north-western corner. The latter could not possibly supply the soldiers' demands for foodstuffs, forage, and other natural materials such as wood for construction and cooking, or leather. A legion of 5,000 men required approximately 7,500 kilos of grain and 450 kilos of fodder per day, or 225 and 13.5 tonnes per month. Some of the soldiers' needs were supplied directly from the imperial centre, but this was cumbersome and logistically problematic in a world where wheat doubled in price for every fifty miles it moved. Wherever possible, it was much better to pay cash and let local suppliers meet the demand: that Secundus' purchase was witnessed by two centurions suggests that he was supplying the military.

After the loss of the Roman general Varus and his three legions in the Battle of the Teutoburg Forest in AD 9 – where a coalition of partly subdued barbarian Germani under the leadership of Arminius managed to reassert their political independence – Rome's expansion into areas east of the Rhine slowly ground to a halt. Further south, the east–west line of the Danube quickly came to form a similar frontier line, and, by the mid-first century, the arc of the two river lines began to mark the broad geographical boundary of the intense economic and cultural provincial development which eventually produced Ausonius and his many peers. But, even if operating with less intensity beyond them, the transformative economic effects of this vast imperial system did not stop at its borders.

Within the broader Roman imperial system, the opportunities for neighbouring populations took two basic forms. One occurred close to the border, on either side: supplying the legions, as the chance survival of the record of Stelos' cow sale reminds us. The second involved longer-distance trade networks, which stretched much further afield into central Europe. Best known is the trade in amber: coagulated sap from ancient, submerged woodlands, much prized by the Mediterranean world for jewellery. The amber washed up on the shores of the southern Baltic and was brought south by designated routes to several points on Rome's Danuban frontier. There was also a constant demand for human labour. While the legions were composed of Roman citizens, half of the army comprised non-citizen auxiliaries, who could be recruited from either side of the frontier. Inscriptions record many recruits from beyond who lived long and prospered in the Roman world, although many others crossed back home in retirement. Alongside this voluntary population flow, there were also well-established slaving networks. Unlike the well-documented Viking-dominated slave trade at the other end of the millennium, the surviving sources are not clear on who was doing the slaving in the Roman period, and from which parts of Europe its victims were generally being taken. But household slaves and extra labour for the fields were in constant demand in a Roman world of high infant mortality (half of all children died before they were five) and low population densities.

The limitations of our available sources make it difficult to explore the effects of the Empire's economic stimulus through the individual lives of those who lived beyond its borders, as we can for the more recent past in the case of the modern West. But the broader archaeological picture that has emerged in recent decades is striking. At the start of the first millennium AD, Europe was divided into three broad zones of distinctly unequal development. The densest populations and largest settlements, reflecting more productive agricultural technologies and more complicated networks of exchange, were located west of the Rhine and south of the Danube. Further east, in a second north-central European zone which ran as far as the river Vistula in modern Poland, more subsistence-level farming supported lower population densities and smaller, more temporary settlements, with little evidence for exchange of any kind. In parts of this region, the only man-made structures in use for more than a single generation or two were cemeteries: these were employed continually and for a variety of purposes, including social gatherings of different types, over several centuries. The prevailing agricultural economy couldn't maintain the fertility of any single set of fields for long enough to generate long-term settlements, so the communities' burial sites provided their most permanent foci. Beyond the Vistula and the outer arc of the Carpathian mountains, the third – outer – zone of Europe was heavily forested with still simpler agricultural regimes, lower population densities, and no sign at all of non-local exchange networks.

Uncovering this broader pattern has made it possible to establish two further points. First, it explains why Roman expansion stopped where it did. As has also been observed in the case of ancient China, empires that depend on arable agricultural production tend to grind to a halt just beyond the point where the productive potential of new territories makes them worth the costs of conquest. The underlying cost-benefit equation holds broadly true, but imperial ambition will push armies a little beyond the net-gain line. In the Roman case, some of our sources comment that Britain wasn't really worth conquering when Claudius sent four legions north of the Channel in AD 43, and it wasn't so much the defeat of Varus – fully avenged over the next decade – as the relative overall poverty of the region between the Rhine and the Elbe that really brought the legions to a halt there. Second, and more important, it allows us to chart the scale of the subsequent revolution generated by three to four hundred years of sustained Roman economic demand in the immediate hinterland of the Empire.

The Romans may have continued to dismiss all their neighbours as barbarians, but a major change gathered momentum. The barely subsistence-level forms of agriculture which prevailed in the second, central north European zone had given way by the fourth century, in a swathe of territory immediately beyond these frontiers, to more productive farming regimes with a much heavier emphasis on grain crops, which generally produce much more food per hectare than stock-raising. This mini agricultural revolution in turn supported much bigger populations, larger, more stable settlements, and healthy agricultural surpluses, some of which were converted into cash and Roman goods at the frontier. Large, permanent villages appear for the first time in this part of Iron Age central Europe from the late first century AD onwards. And so intertwined did its economic relationship with the Empire become subsequently that by the fourth century Roman coins provided an everyday means of exchange in many of its frontier regions: among Germanic tribes including the Gothic Tervingi of the Lower Danube, for instance, and the Alamanni of the Upper Rhine. Roman imports, particularly of wine and olive oil but more mundane items too, are plentiful in the fourth-century remains of this same belt of territory stretching a hundred kilometres and more beyond the defended Roman border. Parts of it even saw a modest but noticeable expansion in craft manufacture and exchange. Local pottery industries, marked by the introduction of the wheel, had grown up in some places, and a brand-new non-Roman glass industry was also servicing demand beyond the frontier. Both industries were clearly following the Roman example, and perhaps even drew directly on Roman expertise. Historical references confirm the continued importance into the fourth century of archaeologically invisible exports – foodstuffs, animals, and labour – going in the other direction, and iron-ore production, too, increased dramatically in certain regions of barbarian Europe, in part to service Roman demand.

Behind this macro-economic transformation stood myriads of small-scale innovators and entrepreneurs, like Stelos, who responded to the economic opportunities presented by unprecedented demand from legionaries by pioneering the more intensive agricultural practices that eventually appeared on both sides of the frontier. Because individual transactions were mainly recorded on perishable materials like wood or papyrus, these individual success stories can't be told, but the archaeological evidence en masse does throw up striking material reflections of the new wealth that was simultaneously flowing into non-Roman societies beyond the frontier, and being generated within them. It is also clear that this new wealth was not being shared equally, at the periphery as at the centre. It's no more than an old nationalist myth that the largely Germanic-speaking populations which dominated much of Europe's zone two at the start of the first millennium were characterized by widespread social equality. The overall impact of the new wealth was to heighten prevailing differences and probably also create some new ones. The social elite of the frontier were customarily buried with the jewellery and clothing accessories they had worn in life, and, over time, these were increasingly made of silver from reworked Roman *denarii*.

Nor were the transformative effects of economic contact with Roman imperialism remotely equal in geographical terms. Europe's third zone, north and east of the Vistula and the Carpathians, was, as far as we can see, so distant from Rome's borders as to be left completely untouched by these transformative processes. Virtually no Roman imports have been found there, nor do its populations figure in any of the narrative action reported in historical sources (although it is possible that some of the slaving networks may have stretched that far beyond the frontier in search of victims). Without highly technical assistance, it's also generally impossible to tell remains of 500 BC from the region apart from those of AD 500. Little or nothing of substance changed in this third zone over the entire millennium covered by Rome's rise and fall.

Within the overall story of development beyond Rome's borders, proximity to the centre was everything. By the fourth century AD, the most intensive evidence for socio-economic transformation within zone two as a whole – as you would expect of a world where transport was so slow and expensive – was limited to an inner imperial periphery, a bit more than 100 kilometres in width, where local populations could respond most effectively to the economic opportunities of Empire. In between this inner periphery and the untouched world of zone three developed an outer periphery stretching another few hundred kilometres from the imperial frontier. Roman imports are present here, but in smaller quantities compared to the inner periphery, and the region was probably a source only of more luxury goods – like amber and people – worth transporting over greater distances, since it was too remote from the frontier to participate in legionary supply networks. Even so, contacts with the Empire were still important enough here to have visible effects. A fascinating glimpse of this has emerged recently in the identification of several hundred kilometres of causeways and roads in the southern hinterland of the Baltic which were constructed in the early centuries AD, presumably to service and control the burgeoning trade in amber (and possibly also in slaves, but there's no way to be sure). It was originally thought that these were likely to be Slavic constructions of the late first millennium, but dendrochronological analysis (dating by tree rings) has produced a secure ascription to the Roman period. The sheer scale of the effort makes clear the overall value of the exchange network that these connections served.

Roman imperial power spread outwards overland from the circle of the Mediterranean, since it lacked any means to transport its legions into other parts of the globe. The same limitation also meant that the long-term operations of the Roman imperial system created by these initial conquests generated relatively simple geographical patterns. Formal conquest radiated outwards from Rome in the centuries either side of the birth of Christ until it ran out of territories worth the price of annexation. Territories within that line then began the slow journey to full provincial status, while, beyond it, there eventually emerged an inner periphery whose populations had sufficient access to the Empire to generate more intensive networks of economic exchange. Beyond that lay an outer periphery, too far away to satisfy any imperial demand which did not involve luxury goods worth the cost and effort of long-distance transport. Still further away, the world beyond the river Vistula had no visible engagement with the Roman system whatsoever.

Modern Western imperialism, by contrast, grew to span the entire globe. Created by powers with the naval and railway-building capacity to construct vast imperial networks, the modern West generated much more complicated geographical patterns. On closer examination, however, its interlocking economic structures operated in ways which largely paralleled its ancient Roman counterpart.

'WE HOLD A VASTER EMPIRE THAN HAS EVER BEEN'

In 1853 a teenage boy left the Gujarati city of Navsari to join his father in Bombay. For generations the Tatas had been Parsi priests in Navsari, but, in the first half of the nineteenth century, Nusserwanji Tata broke the family mould to set up a small export business in Bombay. His son Jamsetji was destined for an English education there, at the new school that would eventually become Elphinstone College. The city, then under British control, was booming. With the Bombay Presidency, the regional headquarters of the East India Company, located there and busily improving transport links throughout the region, the port was expanding rapidly as an important trade hub within the British Empire. After Britain gained control of several Chinese ports in the First Opium War (1839–42), Tata senior had grand ambitions of shipping opium from the Indian region of Malwa into Chinese markets.

In 1859, two years after the widespread Indian Mutiny against British rule, and one year after Britain assumed direct control of the East India Company's assets, Jamsetji turned twenty. His education complete, he was sent to Hong Kong, where he quickly worked out that more money could be made from cotton than opium, and persuaded his father to change focus. The switch proved more profitable than the two could possibly have imagined, when the American Civil War broke out in 1861 and Union forces imposed a blockade on Confederate ports. As the American supply of cotton to British factories dried up, the price of Indian cotton and textile exports rocketed, with revenues into Bombay tripling. This sudden, massive influx of wealth drove up the share prices of Indian textile companies and unleashed a mass of speculative ventures.

Jamsetji was again pressed into action, travelling to Britain in ships loaded with raw cotton, where he quickly established close links with some Lancashire mill owners. From them he gained a deeper understanding of the manufacturing side of the cotton industry. His natural business acumen had been greatly encouraged by the fact that Bombay's business clubs, unlike those in Calcutta, were open to Indian businessmen, facilitating the mutual transfer of practical know-how across racial divides. London's Parsi community had also developed the habit of gathering in a sort of informal club at the home of Dadabhai Naoroji, one of India's leading nationalist intellectuals and later a founding member of the Indian National Congress Party. Between the two, Jamsetji learned the value of networking (to say nothing of the virtues of good political connections) to business success. When he returned to Bombay, he founded his own club: a practice later continued by his son.

By 1869, Jamsetji Tata felt sufficiently confident in his understanding of the broader textile business to buy a bankrupt oil mill in Chinchpokli, south of Bombay. Converting it to cotton, he turned it around and sold it on for a handsome profit. Thus began the family's long and hugely successful involvement in textile manufacturing (as opposed to just exporting raw cotton). Flush with capital from his many successful ventures and having mastered the manufacturing technologies of Lancashire – a knowledge greatly strengthened by his practice of hiring a mix of Indian and English employees – Jamsetji next created a huge mill complex in the city of Nagpur. The site was chosen for its proximity to supplies of cotton and coal, cheaper land prices and the railroad link to Bombay. Selling its products throughout the Empire and generating annual average profits of 20 per cent, the Tata family business mushroomed. Over the next two generations it diversified into iron, steel, engineering and locomotive-building, hydro-electricity, petrochemicals, hotels, printing, insurance, cement and air transport (founding what would later become Air India).

As European empires spread across the planet, from the early modern period onwards, economic opportunities followed in their wake, to be seized by a great many individuals and families like the Tatas. Of these empires, the British was certainly the largest. At its greatest extent, as a famous Canadian Christmas stamp from 1898 so graphically illustrated in splashes of red (see p. 45), it covered almost a quarter of the earth's landmass. But an equivalent French stamp of the same

era would have boasted nearly as much blue, and that's not taking account of older Dutch, Spanish and Portuguese possessions, or the territories recently acquired by relative newcomers such as America, Germany, Belgium and Italy.

The Tatas' success story echoes those of non-Romans in the periphery of that earlier Empire, but several apparent differences jump out when the modern Western imperial edifice is compared to its Roman predecessor, the most obvious of which is starkly illustrated by the postage stamp: scale. Modern Western imperialism was literally global, bringing much of the planet under its direct rule, and nearly all of it into its economic networks in some way, shape, or form. There were some parts of the planet which still remained, to all intents and purposes, outside the imperial system by the twentieth century – vast stretches of the Amazon interior, the highlands of Papua New Guinea, parts of Central Asia – but the tendrils of Western economic power stretched out over a previously inconceivable percentage of the earth's surface. Roman imperialism, on the other hand, was regional: the Mediterranean and much of its immediate hinterland fell under its direct control, and a swathe of territory from north-central Europe to Ukraine participated in its trade networks to greater and lesser degrees. But when you factor in relative speeds of movement, much of this apparent difference evaporates. On its longest diagonal, direct Roman rule stretched the best part of 5,000 kilometres. Given that everything on land in antiquity moved at about one-twentieth of the kind of speeds easily manageable today (p. 17), this is the equivalent of a modern state stretching out over 100,000 kilometres, or two and a half times, more or less, the circumference of the earth (almost exactly 40,000 kilometres). In its own context, the Roman Empire was as much a global power as the empires of the modern West.

A second point of apparent difference is that the Roman Empire formed a continuous block of territory, assembled from the various hinterlands of the Mediterranean basin, whereas the possessions of modern Western powers were dotted in patches of different sizes across the planet. Again, however, there is a deeper similarity in how the two systems operated in practice. The large splotches of red and blue on old colonial maps (and stamps) are in an important sense misleading. At first sight the Tatas might look pretty much like the Vanderbilts, the principal difference being the latter had a head start: Cornelius Vanderbilt was already one of the world's richest men when Jamsetji Tata was just starting to explore the potential of cotton. There are differences between the two family histories, however, which run much deeper than chronology.

Maps and stamps tend to imply that all the empire's subordinated territories existed on the same footing. Britain's territories must all have had the same status because they're all coloured red: likewise those splashes of French blue. This was not the case. The patterns of provincial and peripheral integration into the modern Western Empire, as it had developed up to the outbreak of World War II, closely resembled what had unfolded in and beyond the Roman world in the first three centuries after the birth of Christ. Look behind the red and blue on the maps and a similar, threefold pattern of participation in the imperial system emerges: fully integrated provinces, substantially integrated inner periphery, and much less integrated outer periphery.

PROVINCES AND PERIPHERIES

The modern equivalent to Rome's provinces – the places where, over time, families like that of Ausonius would come to full economic, cultural and political participation in the structures of Empire – were settler colonies. In these areas, the settlers came – through a combination of violence, negotiation, and disease – to compose a majority of the population, and eventually introduced so many European cultural and institutional structures that they effectively became part of an expanded core of the Western Empire, wherever they happened to be placed geographically. The North American home of the Vanderbilts is the most obvious example, and there the rise of what had originally been a provincial community was so dramatic that, by the early twentieth century, it had already become the dominant economic force within the broader Western Empire. But the so-called 'White Dominions' of the British Empire – of which America was originally one – also fall into this category: Canada, Australia and New Zealand. By the early years of the twentieth century, per capita GDP in these now self-governing entities had already surpassed that of the British imperial motherland. None of the other European imperial powers exported enough of their native population to, or generated sufficient wealth within, any of their colonies to set them on a similar long-term trajectory towards membership of the twentieth-century imperial core. France had potentially done so in the case of New France, Acadia and Louisiana, but most of these were brought under British rule in the eighteenth century and all three went on to develop as parts of Canada and the United States.[7]

Beyond this expanded imperial core, by the twentieth century, lay the imperial periphery. As in antiquity its component parts can be split into inner and outer portions, based on the relative values of their direct trade with the Empire. In the Roman case, where exchange largely depended upon land transport, 'inner' and 'outer' also work as geographical descriptors. The inner periphery was simply closer to the borders of Empire as the crow flies: the hundred-kilometre-wide zone immediately beyond the frontier which helped supply the legions and received a host of everyday goods in return. At first sight, the imperial systems of the modern West look very different. Because their territories were linked together by a combination of sea and (increasingly) rail networks, many of the trading partners that belonged to the inner periphery in economic terms were further away from the Western imperial heartland in terms of miles or kilometres than some of their outer peripheral counterparts. Parts of the Indian subcontinent and the Far East, for instance, played a significantly more important role in the trading networks of Empire than did much of Africa, which was physically closer to Europe. But when you look at the maps of Empire a bit more closely, measuring proximity and separation – as you always should – in terms of the time it actually took to cover a particular distance, not the distance itself as measured in absolute miles or kilometres, you quickly find that the periphery of the modern West, as it had developed by the 1920s and 1930s, effectively mirrored its Roman counterpart. Linked by boat and train, the inner imperial periphery was in fact closer to the European heartland of Empire in travel time than its outer counterpart.

In reality, therefore, the imperial shipping and railway timetables of the earlier twentieth century provide a much better guide to the identity of the inner periphery than splashes of red or blue on a map. In part, the inner periphery was composed of formally constituted Western colonies, or more accurately particular regions within such colonies. Cotton from India, gold from South Africa, tea and coffee from British East Africa, rubber from the Far East, sugar from the Caribbean: all were in high demand to service Western needs, and many of these goods were produced in territories under formal imperial control. Other parts of the inner periphery remained politically independent, but again oriented a significant portion of their economic activity to meet imperial demand. In some parts of the globe, this economic integration began at gunpoint: Japan and China were never formal colonies, but in the nineteenth century their markets and natural resources were opened up by force – 'gunboat diplomacy' – with Western imperial powers regularly using brute force to impose their will on militarily weaker states.

What defined both of these kinds of territory as belonging to the inner periphery were the shipping routes and railways. By the early decades of the twentieth century there had emerged a globally connected network of ports, each strategically placed to serve a hinterland rich in the sought-after products of Empire. Originally, these ports had been connected to their hinterlands via river systems, but, starting in the second half of the nineteenth century, an increasingly dense and more convenient network of railway lines (one of which made it possible for Jamsetji Tata to build his cotton mill outside Bombay) began to carry more of the traffic.

As was the case with its Roman counterpart, the total value of the modern inner periphery's trade with the heartland (in proportionate terms) surpassed that of the outer periphery, and generated enough new wealth to kick-start significant processes of socio-economic change. Some of this was driven by European migrants, attracted by the many opportunities for self-enrichment. For the most part, they were concentrated in the commercial and administrative hubs of the cities and in particular in those areas earmarked for European occupation, such as Kenya's White Highlands or the plantations of the West Indies and Dutch East Indies. But, unlike those colonies set on a trajectory to full provincial status, European immigrants here never amounted to more than a small percentage of the total population.

The bulk of production in the inner periphery was undertaken, instead, by indigenous actors, who were sometimes drawn into the imperial export economy by price incentives and commercial opportunities. The modern-day equivalents of Stelos included not just the very grand, like Nusserwanji and Jamsetji Tata, but untold millions of individuals, forgotten to all but their families, who migrated to the inner periphery in search of new opportunities. The less fortunate elements of the indigenous population found that they had no choice. Many colonial regimes operated forced-labour laws, which they used on public-works projects – like the railways and roads – or at times to supplement the labour force on European farms (as in French West Africa). Slavery, of course, was used for a long time to run the plantation economies of the Americas, and even after its formal abolition, types of slavery in all but name continued to be used, especially in the rubber plantations of the Belgian Congo. Colonial tax regimes requiring payment in the currency of the imperial power could also force producers to orient their production to imperial markets. This mechanism was deployed to build the plantation sector in the Dutch East

Indies, while in British and French Africa hut and poll taxes were used to cover the cost of colonial administration while also bolstering the imperial currency (since all the tax revenues were deposited in the central banks of the mother countries).

Over time, this potent combination of voluntary and involuntary economic participation substantially changed both population and wealth distribution across the inner periphery. Aside from making the fortunes of many Europeans and smaller numbers of indigenous businessmen, such as the Tatas, one larger, structural effect had become very marked by the inter-war period: relocation. In India, cities like Bombay were already doubling their populations every decade by the mid-nineteenth century, while its opium- and cotton-producing hinterlands sucked in labour in vast quantities. These effects were mirrored right across the inner periphery, around the treaty ports of imperial China and Japan, in the regions of French settlement in Algeria, and the plantation colonies of the Caribbean, as more and more of the population relocated closer to the coastal ports or to the river and railway networks which connected them to the interior production zones.

The outer periphery, by contrast, was marked by lower volumes of direct trade with the core's economic system. Lacking either resources or markets for which imperial producers hungered, or an ecology that made it possible for imperial administrators to implement large-scale export-crop farming, these areas – even if under formal colonial rule – attracted less investment in transport infrastructure and remained relatively isolated in geographical terms. Across much of the outer periphery, most people seldom if ever encountered a white person, even if their homes were coloured red or blue on the maps. All the same, many people living in this outer periphery still found the patterns of their lives being substantially remade as imperial trade networks increased in intensity over time.

Towns in the interior often dried up, lacking convenient access to the export trade to Europe and North America. In one extreme case, Timbuktu went from a wealthy, populous entrepôt on an ancient trans-Saharan trade route to almost total extinction when French roads and railways reoriented trade laterally along the coast. Now used proverbially in the West for a place as remote as it is possible to be, Timbuktu was once the hugely wealthy centre of a vast web of commerce. More generally, even when not themselves drawn physically into the inner periphery, agricultural producers in the outer periphery sometimes supplied food crops to consumers there, particularly when the latter, in shifting their production to export crops or leaving agriculture behind altogether, lost the ability fully to feed themselves. Colonial territories like Upper Volta or Mali, nominally independent states like Bhutan and Lesotho, and even large areas in the interiors of India or China, whose social and economic organization saw little change before World War II, all effectively operated in the outer imperial periphery. There was a small amount of exchange between Bhutan and British India, and some substantial labour migration from Upper Volta, Mali and Lesotho to the farms and mines in the neighbouring territories that *were* linked into the global economy. Gross output and per capita income in the outer periphery did sometimes rise on the back of this trade, but generally much less than in the inner periphery, which in turn rose less than the provinces.

As a consequence, most peripheral societies – inner and outer – witnessed much slower processes of economic transformation up to 1939 than the Western Empire's provinces. In practice, the boundaries between all three categories could fluctuate, and did not always correspond neatly to the borders drawn on maps. Different regions within the same jurisdiction might belong to the inner and outer periphery, as was certainly the case in China and India. South Africa, arguably, contained all three elements of the imperial system in one: a provincial core in areas of substantial white settlement and its major cities, an inner periphery in some mining and exporting agricultural areas, and an outer periphery in areas which effectively functioned as labour reserves for what would after 1948 become the apartheid economy. Nevertheless, as was the case for Rome's neighbours, the consequences of any level of integration into the imperial economy proved revolutionary for all concerned.

In some cases, the overall impact was severely negative. After China's forced opening to the West, its economy fell backwards. Over the course of the nineteenth century, when Britain's per capita income more than doubled, China's dropped by a tenth. Even if individual fortunes were still being made within China's territories in the later nineteenth and early twentieth centuries, the overall effect was a century of crisis. But this kind of absolute decline was not the normal macro-economic outcome in either the inner or outer periphery. India was more typical. Its economy grew, just at a slower pace than those of the core provinces of the imperial system. This provided new opportunities for those, like the Tatas, able and astute enough to grasp them, but the economy as a whole fell relative to that of the imperial mother country, while the grandees of the British East India Company utterly ransacked their new possessions, stripping it of jewels and other forms of moveable wealth as they constructed vast personal fortunes (filling the country mansions they constructed back at home with much of the loot). The long-term economic development in the periphery had a significance, however, which went far beyond the limited rise of indigenous business classes or the remaking of prevailing patterns of demography and production. Even when not immediately apparent, any major economic change, by dint of redistributing wealth, will necessarily have far-reaching political consequences.

4

The Power of Money

Early on the morning of 11 September 1973 a car raced through the streets of Santiago. A short while earlier, Chilean President Salvador Allende had received a phone call alerting him to a naval mutiny in the port city of Valparaiso. When he rang his Army Commander for news, General Augusto Pinochet said he'd investigate and phone back. A few minutes of silence was enough to make the president realize that Pinochet wasn't going to be calling. Scrambling to alert his allies that a coup was underway, Allende rushed towards the presidential palace.

The president's attempt to build a Chilean socialist utopia had always been perilous. He'd won the 1970 election with barely a third of the vote. This was sufficient under the Chilean electoral system to gain him the presidency, but with a weak mandate and only minority support in an unsympathetic Congress. The economy he inherited, if not sickly, still gave him little with which to build a new Jerusalem, persistently high inflation running alongside steady but unspectacular growth. Aiming to kick-start a transformation, Allende's initial programme of generous spending unleashed a short-term boom, but by 1973 the economy was running aground. Production fell, inflation soared, rolling strikes broke out, and queues for bread grew steadily longer. Despite this alarming situation, with domestic discontent on the rise, Chile's military clung to its traditional professionalism, holding back from the political intervention so characteristic of other Latin American generals. What finally pushed Pinochet into action was American backing.

Even by the standards of American presidents, Richard Nixon detested all things communist. In the late 1960s, the previous Chilean government had embarked on a dramatic programme of social reform, involving land redistributions and the partial nationalization of an American-owned copper industry. This tested Nixon's patience, but for as long as Chile stayed aligned with the West, Washington grinned and bore it. Allende, however, pushed his luck. Not only did he complete the nationalization process without further compensation to US interests, but he threatened to move Chile into a Soviet orbit. For Washington, this was too much. The United States was still smarting over the loss of Cuba to the communist camp after the 1959 revolution and was not about to tolerate a second socialist state in its backyard. Through covert activities that included secretly funding anti-Allende politicians and media, placing pressure on the Chilean military (where US intelligence agents found sympathetic officers), and encouraging responses to the first whispers of a coup in Santiago's corridors of power, the White House made clear that it would welcome Allende's downfall.

By the end of the day, Allende was dead by his own hand and Pinochet in charge of a military junta. He would go on to govern Chile for the next seventeen years. Although the CIA's involvement in Allende's overthrow and effective execution sparked liberal indignation across the world, the Nixon administration was acting within well-defined parameters of Western imperial power. After World War II, the gunboat diplomacy of the nineteenth and early twentieth centuries had generally given way to a new type of dominance. Because so many developing countries were so economically dependent on the new Western Empire, its leaders, particularly the United States, could exert enormous influence by less overtly intrusive methods. The toolbox for dealing with recalcitrant governments was extensive: cutting off aid, stonewalling trade negotiations, supporting their domestic enemies, imposing travel sanctions on leaders, and freezing bank accounts. And if none of this was enough, then, as in Chile, covert action could help install a more compliant regime. Salvador Allende was only one in a long list of rulers in the West's imperial periphery post-1945, like Iran's Mohammad Mossadegh or Guatemala's Jacobo Arbenz, who were deposed when they became too assertive, and threatened Western hegemony. Many others, well aware of these examples and reluctant to antagonize the West, tempered any initial hostility or even actively courted Western patronage by serving as reliable allies or proxies, as did Ferdinand Marcos of the Philippines and Mobutu Sese Seko of Zaire (now the Democratic Republic of Congo). All of which bears a remarkable resemblance to how the late Roman Empire came to control its own inner periphery.

CHNODOMARIUS AND MACRIANUS

During the first three centuries AD, populations beyond Rome's Rhine and Danube frontiers used some of their new wealth to import a wide range of Roman goods. Trade links were one source of this wealth, but not the only one. Over the centuries, thousands of individuals had returned home from Roman military service with their savings and retirement bonuses (p. 38). Further up the social scale, diplomatic subsidies were systematically used by Roman emperors to support client kings who were willing to rule their own parts of the frontier broadly in accord with Roman interests. Called 'annual gifts' in our sources, these sometimes took the form of fine clothing and exotic foodstuffs as well as cash payments, some of which the kings then recycled to firm up support at home. In the less official economy raiding, too, was endemic (and quite probably sanctioned sometimes by the same client kings, who were perfectly capable of playing a double game). The Roman economy, despite all the expansion beyond the frontier (Chapter 3), remained significantly more developed than its barbarian peripheries, and the huge variety of its products provided highly attractive targets for acquisitive eyes particularly in the inner periphery, where the frontier was easy to cross. In 1967, gravel-digging in the Rhine near the Roman city of Speyer led to the discovery of the looted bounty of a Roman villa. Late in the third century, some raiders had ransacked the villa, and tried to get their booty back across the river in carts loaded onto rafts. But these had come to grief, probably sunk by Roman patrol boats. The carts contained an extraordinary 700 kilos of stolen goods, including every piece of metalwork the raiders could lay their hands on: not just silver plate from the dining room, but a mass of kitchen utensils including fifty-one cauldrons, twenty-five bowls and basins, and twenty iron ladles, not to mention all the villa's agricultural equipment. Any and every piece of Roman metalwork could be reused or recycled on the other side of the frontier, where there was always a use for looted goods and metal was in constant demand. By the fourth century these wealth-generating contacts with the Roman world – peaceful and otherwise – had been growing in intensity for three hundred years, and their revolutionary effect upon Rome's neighbours became only too visible.

In 357 the armed followers of an Alamannic confederation led by an ambitious overking by the name of Chnodomarius faced up to the Roman forces of the Western Caesar (junior emperor) Julian, close to the modern city of Strasbourg. The Alamanni occupied a block of territory immediately beyond Rome's Upper Rhine and Upper Danube frontiers, ruled by a series of local princes, over whom Chnodomarius had established a degree of hegemony. In the early 350s Chnodomarius exploited an imperial civil war to advance his own expansionist agenda, seizing a strip of land on the Roman side of the frontier. As battle commenced, Chnodomarius led 35,000 men, Julian 13,000, but the Alamanni suffered a devastating defeat. Their leader was captured along with his retinue, and 6,000 of their men died on the battlefield, many cut down as they struggled to get back across the Rhine. The Romans reportedly lost only 247 men. Especially given the similarity in names, you could be forgiven for thinking that nothing had changed in the four hundred years since Julius Caesar. His mid-first century BC first-hand account of the Gallic Wars, the *Commentarii de Bello Gallico*, is full of one-sided confrontations, with equally catastrophic outcomes for Rome's enemies. What happened after this fourth-century battle, however, clearly illustrates how much the world beyond Rome had changed.

In the first century BC, or indeed AD, such a defeat would have caused the total destruction of the enemy confederation involved. This happened in the case of the Suebic king Ariovistus, a former Roman ally, whose confederation fell apart completely after its defeat by Julius Caesar in 58 BC, its leader never heard of again. Even in victory, Germanic alliances of this era tended to collapse. In AD 9 the Cheruscian chief Arminius ('Hermann the German') put together a confederation which ambushed and destroyed three whole Roman legions and their supporting auxiliary troops – well over 20,000 men – in the Teutoburg forest (p. 37). Despite this stunning victory, his coalition quickly unravelled and he himself was betrayed and killed. The underlying explanation for the widespread political instability of the early Germanic-speaking world is not at all complicated. The relatively small area of north-central Europe they occupied (zone two of the European landscape as it stood at the birth of Christ: p. 39) was home to between fifty and sixty different political units in the first century AD. As such an order of magnitude indicates, each of these units was small, and many of them were not under the control of strongly established central leaders ('kings') but run by looser councils of chieftains. This reflected the region's general economic under-development, and meant that large-scale, stable political authority was simply impossible. Coalitions could be assembled, but were always going to fall apart – in victory or defeat – once their immediate aims had been achieved.

By the mid-fourth century, however, even such an apparently catastrophic defeat as the battle of Strasbourg was not remotely the end of the Alamannic confederation, which quickly regrouped politically and was soon ready to fight again. Within a decade, another Roman army faced another large Alamannic force, at the battle of Chalons in 364. It was another Roman victory, if this time with heavier casualties: 1,100 Roman soldiers died. And still, the Alamannic confederation continued to exist, throwing up another preeminent overking in the second half of the decade, Macrianus, who quickly became the chief object of Roman military and diplomatic pressure. Nor were the Alamanni an exception. It was exactly the same much further east, at the mouth of the Danube. There another large political confederation, dominated by the Gothic Tervingi, controlled the region immediately beyond Rome's defended frontier line. The Tervingi had risen to prominence in the 310s, before suffering a heavy defeat at the hands of the Emperor Constantine in 332. Again, however, defeat did not prompt dissolution. Under a series of leaders from the same ruling dynasty, the Tervingi remained the dominant force in the region. Right across the inner periphery in the late-Roman period (p. 40), the same overall change is apparent. The tangled multiplicity of chieftains and councils documented in the first centuries BC and AD had given way to a smaller number of larger, more durable political confederations with much more powerful central leaderships.

In a general sense, this greater political stability was one product of the wealth and larger populations which had collected in the inner periphery through centuries of transformative interaction with the Roman Empire. But the evidence suggests that contact with the Empire was responsible for driving forward this political transformation in some more specific ways. By the fourth century AD, in every single branch of the ancient Germanic language group, whose speakers predominated along most of Rome's European frontier line, an older vocabulary of more consensual political leadership had given way to new titles derived from words meaning military command. Where once rulers had titles meaning 'leader of the people', they were now all 'warband leader'. There is every reason to think that this was no coincidence.

In 1955 some Danish workmen were cutting a drainage ditch at Ejsbol Mose in northern Schleswig when they found, in one small section of it, an amazing haul of 600 metallic objects. Nine years and 1,700 square metres later, archaeologists had identified several different deposits thrown into what had once been a shallow lake. The largest was the complete equipment of a well-organized military force from around the year AD 300. It comprised about two hundred spearmen (the excavators found 193 barbed javelin heads and another 187 spearpoints from thrusting lances), of whom maybe a third were also equipped with swords (they found sixty-three belt-sets, together with sixty of the swords and sixty-two of the knives the belts had originally held). At first, the excavators thought they'd uncovered the world's largest known cache of Roman swords, but the reality was even more interesting. Some of the swords were imported, but most turned out to be the work of local producers directly copying Roman manufacturers.

This find, and others like it, make clear that imperial contact did not create new wealth which was shared equally among those living in its periphery. Rather, long-term interaction with the Empire had concentrated greater wealth and advanced military technology among particular groups. Diplomatic subsidies, the tolls exacted on trade goods, pay for military service, the profits from slave-trading (which required the exercise of force), even the booty from successful cross-border raiding: all of this new wealth fell disproportionately into the hands of those with established military capacity, particularly in the inner periphery but to some extent in the outer periphery too. It also gave them the means to develop their military potential further, both by hiring more warriors and purchasing superior equipment.

These developments accentuated some existing features of north-central European society. When Rome arrived on its doorstep, this corner of what the Romans called barbarian Europe was already substantially militaristic and far from egalitarian. But new flows of Roman wealth provided a mechanism for particular leaders, through internal competition and an extended arms race, to build up the more durable power structures that are evident in the larger and more lasting confederations Rome was facing across the frontier by the fourth century. Sometimes this competition had brutal outcomes. The equipment found in Ejsbol Mose had all been smashed prior to being thrown in the lake: a ritual sacrifice which made its investigators (reasonably) suppose that a similar fate had probably also been suffered by its recent owners. But on other occasions, perhaps more often, competitive confrontation led to the creation of new alliances where weaker parties accepted the effective overkingship of an acknowledged stronger neighbour.

The reasoning here is straightforward. All the documented new confederations were alliances between formerly separate military leaders. This kind of relationship left many of the junior partners in positions of intermediate authority, retaining direct control of their own bodies of soldiery. All the same, the overall political effect was dramatic. Transformative contact with the Empire had generated mutually reinforcing processes of militarization and political centralization, driven forward by those groups in the periphery who were best positioned to exploit the opportunities for acquiring new wealth and advanced military hardware from the Roman world. As a result, relations between the Roman Empire and its fourth-century inner periphery shifted substantially, moving away from the legionary gunboat diplomacy of the early period.

The new confederations had first made their presence felt in the mid-third century, when their aggressive ambitions and extra military power inflicted some immediate losses on the Empire. This was the period in which northern Britain and Belgium suffered so much damage that settlement densities there failed to recover even in the Golden Age of the fourth century (p. 17). Roman villas were large, undefended manor houses, so that if security collapsed in any sector of the frontier line, they would always be an opposition confederation's target of choice, guaranteeing localized economic disruption in the affected region as these agricultural estates ceased to function. More strategically, the confederations' greater military capacity also forced adjustments to the placement of Rome's European frontier lines. Some areas which had been on a trajectory to full Roman provincial status found themselves abandoned to the inner periphery, with Roman soldiery and administration withdrawn. The single largest loss was Transylvanian Dacia beyond the Danube, but the northern tip of Roman Britain beyond Hadrian's Wall was given up too, as were the *Agri Decumates*, a region between the Upper Rhine and Danube which was occupied by the Alamanni. These territories were surrendered in the face of generally increasing outside military pressure from the new confederations, but the final act in each instance seems to have been a calculated withdrawal of Roman soldiers and administrators.

At the same time, the new confederations of the inner periphery also offered Rome some useful opportunities. By the fourth century, the Empire was regularly drawing on their military capacity: allied contingents from the Gothic Tervingi served on three separate imperial campaigns against Persia, with similar warrior groups from the Alamanni and Franks on the Rhine being drafted in for campaigns by Western emperors. Such contingents had to be paid (putting still more wealth in the hands of dominant military groups) and the numbers involved were not vast, but they were much cheaper than recruiting extra Roman soldiers, since they went home after each campaign. All the same, once the necessary adjustments had been made, fourth-century Rome was able to assert and retain a marked dominance, despite the greater levels of military and political organization that can be observed among the new confederations.

As Chnodomarius found to his cost, none of the new confederations was powerful enough to challenge Roman military might directly. Even where tensions with Rome built up, as they tended to periodically, since ambitious warrior overkings had political agendas of their own, set-piece military confrontations like Strasbourg remained rare. Rome's frontier partners were well aware of the likely outcome, and tended not to push their resistance to the point of open confrontation (even if they might encourage, and profit from, a little illicit raiding). Generally speaking, therefore, the course of relations on the later Empire's European frontiers followed a different pattern. About once a political generation (every twenty-five years or so) in the late third and fourth centuries, Roman emperors mounted large-scale expeditions on the far side of each of the four main sectors of the European frontier line (Lower Rhine, Upper Rhine, Middle Danube and Lower Danube). At these moments, some of the Empire's less fortunate neighbours saw their houses burned down in campaigns of terror, the occupants rounded up and sold into slavery. This initial demonstration of military might was usually enough to make the local warlords present themselves in formal submission. The emperor then used these moments of maximum political leverage to rearrange the shape of local confederation politics to suit Roman interests. The life expectancy of the new settlement was extended by exacting high-status hostages, who were hauled off to court for a Roman education, and by granting those who came into line valuable trade deals and annual diplomatic gifts and subsidies, which gave the subordinated partners every reason to preserve the settlement. This combination of stick and carrot was generally enough to maintain broad peace on any frontier sector for the next few decades, with any overly amb-itious king in the meantime likely to find himself removed either by kidnap or targeted assassination (bringing Salvador Allende again inescapably to mind).

This is not to say that everything ran smoothly. Such settlements minimized but did not eliminate cross-border raiding. Different imperial regimes also sometimes arbitrarily changed the policy mix to further their own political agendas. In the early 360s, Valentinian I wanted to appear tough on barbarians, so he unilaterally lowered annual subsidies to the Alamanni and started building forts where it had been agreed there would be none. The result was a serious out-burst of frontier violence, despite Julian's recent (and effective) subjugation of the Upper Rhine frontier region after the battle of Strasbourg. Outside events could also force an emperor's hand. By the late 360s, Valentinian's chief anxiety on the Upper Rhine had become, as we have seen, the rise of a new Alamannic overking: Macrianus. The emperor first tried to organize his assassination, then sent in a special snatch squad to kidnap him. Neither worked, and when serious trouble broke out on another sector of the frontier, Valentinian was forced to change tack. Macrianus was invited to a summit on a ship in the middle of the Rhine and the two reached a deal: Valentinian recognized Macrianus' status as overking of the Alamanni, and granted him favourable terms, in return for which he kept peace on the frontier and directed his expansionary ambitions towards his northern Frankish neighbours.

All of these, however, were relatively minor hiccups. The new military-political confederations had forced a general shift in imperial policy towards manipulative diplomacy, but Rome retained its dominant position. The frontier dynasts wanted to maximize their positions, but few dared to challenge Roman might directly. Peripheral development imposed some constraints on the exercise of imperial dominance but did not reverse it. Even the ambitious Macrianus was so pleased with his special deal that he remained a reliable ally for the rest of his life. Later, Rome's modified approach to the exercise of imperial power found strong echoes, many years later, as the twentieth century unfolded.

OUT OF INDIA (AND AFRICA . . .)

In the later eighteenth and nineteenth centuries, the monarchic rule characteristic of the emergent Western Empire was challenged and partly overturned by a new doctrine. This doctrine held that authority came not from above, but from below: from the people who constituted the nation. It quickly empowered many American colonials to throw off direct British (and Spanish, and Portuguese) imperial control, and the population of France to rise up against homegrown monarchs. In due course nationalism provided ideological justification for further periodic political unrest right across Europe throughout the nineteenth and earlier twentieth centuries. It would also take hold in many of the populations living in the periphery of the European empires under colonial rule: not least in the jewel of the British imperial crown.

European imperialism always provoked local resistance, and its massive expansion in the nineteenth century was no exception. The Zulu wars, the 'Mad' Mahdi of Sudan, the Boxer Rebellion, Diponegro's war of resistance in Dutch Java, Samory Toure's fight with the French in West Africa: on it goes. These uprisings always inflicted losses, sometimes severe ones, but generally met the same fate as Boudicca's assault on Roman rule in Britain, and for much the same reason. The forces resisting imperial expansion were comparatively small, technologically less developed and administratively weak. After their inevitable defeats, pre-colonial elites usually faded into political irrelevance, their places taken by new groups who successfully mastered the practices and technologies of Empire, and, sometimes, too, elements of the culture and rhetoric of its European core: not least the clarion call of national independence.

One of the earliest colonial nationalist movements emerged in India, at the back end of the nineteenth century. As was often the pattern elsewhere, it originated in clubs and salons (partly copied from colonial models) where an indigenous middle class congregated. British India, like many territories of the inner periphery, had a numerically large community of European settlers and administrators, but, as a share of the total population, it amounted only to a tiny capstone on a pyramid of political power that was staffed almost entirely by local recruits. The cost, in both money and manpower, of transposing an entire apparatus of colonial administration from the 'mother country' would have rendered the enterprise economically unviable. Britain sent only the highest officials and officers to India, otherwise recruiting the remainder of its staff and middle management locally, at much less cost. That's how Britain could rule 300 million Indians with just 4,000 civil servants, or how several million people in the interior of West Africa could be governed by ten French officials. As a result, and to maintain a position of superiority that had been originally established by violence and intimidation, the British administration in India, like most other imperial administrations in most parts of the colonized periphery, operated as an effective caste system, with the pinnacle of status and power reserved for Europeans. They recreated some of the institutions of home, like the clubs and schools which dotted Bombay, and even occasionally assimilated members of the local elite into their ranks. But there was never the slightest doubt in colonial societies as to where true power lay.

At first, Bombay's businessmen kept a tactful distance from the developing nationalist conversations. These were for the most part the preserve of India's growing cadre of middle-class intellectuals, who partly overlapped with the senior echelons of indigenous administrators. For the most part, the Indian business community remained pragmatic, showing little ideological commitment to the bubbling nationalist cause as they prospered from the trade networks of Empire. The Tatas, now one of Bombay's most dynamic and successful families, were no exception. Even though Jamsetji Tata was personally close to some of the key thinkers and organizers of the Indian National Congress movement, he himself flew below the political radar, willing to work with the colonial administration. Tata thrived to such an extent in the circles of Empire that he and his sons even entered its centre in triumph: Dorabji went to Cambridge and then joined his brother Ratan in obtaining a knighthood.

In the longer term, however, the political position of the Tatas more closely resembles that of one of the client-rulers of Rome's fourth-century inner periphery, whose children were often taken off to the imperial court as hostages, rather than the Ausonii or Vanderbilts who merged seamlessly into the imperial ruling class. There they were given Roman educations and treated with every possible courtesy, but only for as long as the current diplomatic settlement held. Unlike Ausonius or the Vanderbilts, marriage into the upper social echelons of the Empire was not an option (either for princes of the Alamanni or for the Tatas), and as subsequent developments made clear, they were welcome in the imperial fold only for as long as they did not threaten the interests of those much closer to the centre of imperial power.

By the late nineteenth century, Bombay's mill-owners were starting to look like potential rivals in the eyes of their Lancastrian counterparts. As a result, members of the Indian business community who had seen themselves as equal subjects within a great imperial system discovered that some of the key attributes of 'Britishness' did not apply to them. Tata's own nationalism was first aroused, for example, in 1894, when Britain imposed a duty on Indian cotton, at which point he complained bitterly, if privately to colleagues, about the 'false Imperialism that only had regard for the Englishman'.

All the same, for the next few decades nationalism continued to enjoy a stronger appeal among India's intellectuals and civil servants, who faced more immediate roadblocks to personal ambition, since political power was still ultimately reserved for officials from the mother country. Nationalist leaders with no substantial business interests felt freer to experiment with radical ideologies. The Indian National Congress was no exception, attracting its fair share of socialists, who after World War I were drawn to the Turkish state-led model of capitalism and Soviet central-planning. And as Congress grew increasingly radical, the Bombay business class tempered its support, encouraged by a colonial administration which was trying to win friends where it could. But in the 1930s, partly under the impact of more conservative leaders with closer ties to prominent Indian business families, Congress softened its socialist rhetoric again. This happened at exactly the same moment the imperial government was ramping up protectionist policies in favour of Lancastrian mill-owners, who were struggling amid the Great Depression. The coincidence finally cemented bonds between Indian business and the Congress: the start of a beautiful friendship. Congress gained financial backing for its political campaigns, while business looked forward to reaping due benefit from the state-led industrial policy that Congress was already planning for the country's independence.

India possessed an ancient civilization with powerful indigenous cultural traditions which, especially when mobilized alongside the profits of Empire accrued by its business communities, was able to generate an effective nationalist movement at an early date. But its basic patterns were a recurring feature of the renewed anti-colonial agitation which was affecting large tracts of the old European empires by the mid-twentieth century. Much of it was driven by indigenous professional classes, often composed of educated but structurally sub-ordinated civil servants and managers, seeking to break the glass ceiling that blocked their path to the top. In inner peripheral contexts, increasingly prosperous but still partly marginalized business classes provided natural allies, anticipating the post-independence profits that favourable government policies might push in their direction.

Over the long term, therefore, the inner peripheries of both the ancient Roman and the modern Western imperial systems experienced similar patterns of political upheaval, by respectively the mid-fourth century and the interwar period of the twentieth. If on nothing like the same scale as in the fully enfranchised provinces which eventually entered into the original imperial core, enough new wealth was collected in the hands of particular groups in both the ancient and modern inner peripheries to generate an irresistible change in prevailing patterns of political power: both within the peripheries themselves, and in the overall balance of power between those peripheries and the imperial centre. New wealth always remakes existing balances of power, throwing up new power blocs with both the ability and the need to assert their interests.

In the Roman era, where the powerful social class in the periphery was already substantially militarized, the link between wealth and power was very direct. Cornering a significant percentage of the new wealth accumulating in the periphery both required the application of existing force and increased military capacity further, making it possible for successful leaders to support more warriors and to provide them with the superior equipment becoming available through Roman contacts. In the nineteenth and earlier twentieth centuries it was a combination of wealth, assertive new ideologies, and administrative know-how, rather than mere military capacity, which empowered emerging indigenous elites.

But the overall political effect was comparable: it brought to the fore new indigenous forces that were better able to counter the continued exercise of direct imperial power. And if military capacity was not so central to the modern process of peripheral political evolution as it had been to the ancient one, two world wars nonetheless played a directly catalytic role in the nationalist-cum-independence movements of the modern inner periphery. During these periods of unprecedented conflict, imperial governments were preoccupied by events in Europe while simultaneously making heavy demands upon their colonial resources. Over both world wars, for instance, France sent several hundred thousand subjects from its African colonies on to the battlefield, while Britain recruited over two million soldiers from India alone. The temporary de facto weakening of imperial power between 1914 and 1918 occurred at a point when nationalist movements were for the most part still embryonic. But by the time World War II exploded, many nationalist movements were sufficiently well-established to exploit the problems facing the imperial centre – nowhere more so than in India. Already in the 1930s, Mahatma Gandhi in particular had helped build India's National Congress movement into a broad-based, coherent and well-organized force, capable of the kind of widespread if peaceful civil protest which characterized the famous Salt March of 1930. Over twenty-four days and 240 miles the Salt March challenged the imperial administration's monopoly control of salt supplies, failing in its immediate objectives but ultimately succeeding in transforming the independence movement into a broad-based popular cause, as well as winning it considerable sympathy abroad. Much as Winston Churchill wanted to ignore Gandhi, whom he snidely dismissed as a 'half-naked fakir', he had no option but to negotiate with him and the movement he had stirred.

Against this backdrop of an inner periphery which was already becoming more assertive, the shake-out in the global imperial order caused by World War II had a substantial impact on the push for independence in the colonies. After the second massive conflict in a generation, the old European empires were faced with colossal and unprecedented levels of public debt, needing both substantial bailouts to fund reconstruction at home and to reduce their annual outgoings. But the only ready source of cash was the United States. America was willing to provide funds in principle, but – as befitted its history as the first colony to throw off European imperial rule – was absolutely not willing to bankroll what it considered outdated imperial ambitions. Along with its rival, the Soviet Union, the US had for decades been championing the principle of self-determination against the right of conquest that underpinned Europe's colonial heritage (provided, of course, that those seeking self-determination weren't in America's own backyard).

The British, French and Dutch all wanted to keep their empires, and in some cases went to war to retake (or attempt to retake) colonies pushing for independence. However, they found after 1945 that the balance of cost and benefit – partly financial, partly ideological – had now swung strongly against retaining direct control of large portfolios of colonies. Home-grown nationalist movements were now better able to mobilize enough support among local populations, justifying themselves through their recent contributions to the collective imperial war effort, to make many of the West's colonies increasingly difficult and hence expensive to govern. Besides, American money talked. The $15 billion in Marshall Aid which America doled out (worth roughly ten times that much in today's money), supplemented by extensive private American investment in Europe and unfettered access to America's markets, was essential to European countries looking to restore their shattered economies. Add to all that determined American non-cooperation with such continued imperial adventures as the British and French attempt to take back the Suez Canal from Egypt in 1956, and the writing was on the wall for old-style European imperialism. More and less voluntarily, and more and less peacefully, the Western powers handed over direct control of their colonies in the decades after 1945 to local elites who had grown strong in the imperial era.

But while this historical progression might initially seem to fit a happy narrative of American exceptionalism, with the first nation to throw off the yoke of British imperialism then assisting others to do the same, that is only half the story. In reality, the process of formal decolonization did not represent so much the end of Western imperialism as its re-expression in a new and highly creative form. Just as the Roman imperial system had adapted its operations to take account of the more powerful confederations that its own operations had generated, while still exercising ultimate control, even amidst decolonization the Western imperial system continued to dominate, via new mechanisms, the vast majority of its old colonial periphery. The institutional structure underpinning this climactic phase of Western imperialism emerged from lengthy discussions, chaired by the Americans, in a small New Hampshire town in the summer of 1944.

BRETTON WOODS

In July of that year, as Allied forces struggled to break out of the
Normandy beachhead and World War II entered its final act, the US
government assembled its allies in the resort town of Bretton Woods.
The purpose was to draw up a blueprint for the financial architecture
of the post-war world. Two men loomed large: John Maynard Keynes
represented Britain, Harry Dexter White the United States. Working
quietly together over the previous two years, they had reached broad
agreement on many issues but were stuck on a main point of difference. Both agreed on the need for a single standard currency in which
all world trade would now be conducted so as to promote a much
greater fluidity of exchange than in the pre-war Depression years,
and that this currency needed to be backed by gold to ensure stability
and trust. But Keynes wanted to restore the status quo ante to the
greatest extent possible. If Britain kept its empire, its colonies would
conduct their external trade in pounds sterling, and bank their
reserves in London, helping to maintain the pound's long-established
role as one of the world's principal reserve currencies. This would
have the additional advantage of keeping down the cost of borrowing in the UK by swelling the pool of money in the British banking
system, allowing Britain to rely on its own resources to fund post-
war reconstruction. White, however, wanting to shift the centre of
global finance to the United States, championed the merits of the US
dollar. To provide the necessary assurance, he proposed fixing its
exchange rate against the stash of gold bullion held at the US's secure
bunker in Fort Knox, which then housed roughly four-fifths of the
world's gold reserves.[8]

   In the end, White got his way. It didn't help Keynes that his health
was failing, but the cards were anyway stacked against him. America
was effectively paying most of the immediate bills of war, and it also
enjoyed a temporary but huge structural advantage. Given the widespread destruction of Europe's economic base, when the war ended
the US accounted for a third of the world's overall output and half its
industrial production. This meant that everyone was eager to get their
hands on American goods, especially the capital goods they needed to

rebuild their homes, factories and infrastructure. This in turn neces-
sitated obtaining so many American dollars that countries quickly
found it most convenient to transact business among themselves in
that currency too, even after their economies began to recover.

The resulting Bretton Woods agreements created a series of institutions to ensure that the post-war global economy would operate
with as few limitations as possible to trade and capital flows, while
protecting the continued dominance of the Western powers. First up,
the General Agreement on Tariffs and Trade (GATT) committed
member states to a regime of tariff reductions that would prevent the
world returning to the closed economies of the Depression years by
gradually scaling down how much governments could tax imports.
Second, the International Monetary Fund (IMF) was created as a
global rainy-day fund, into which member states would pay annual
contributions. If they encountered short-term balance-of-payment
shortages, during which they imported more than they exported and
thus ran out of dollars, they could dip into the Fund for assistance.
And if their payment difficulties proved more intractable, the IMF
would step in as a creditor of last resort, offering more substantial
loans in return for the implementation of a prescribed set of financial
remedies. Needless to say, the fund was not designed to bankroll
socialist utopias. The conference's final brainchild was the World
Bank. Originally intended to fund the reconstruction of war-ravaged
Europe, the Bank soon turned its attention to capitalist development
in the periphery, as the new states emerging from post-war decolonization started knocking on its door. Rounding out the new world
order was the United Nations. Created separately from the Bretton
Woods' financial regime in 1945, it nevertheless helped enshrine the
dominance of the Allied powers and was headquartered – lest there
be any doubt about the new centre of Empire – in New York.

Just two years after the war's conclusion, India declared independence, kick-starting decolonization across the British, French and
Dutch empires. But while few of these new post-colonial nations had
attended the Bretton Woods Conference,[9] nearly all signed up to its
institutional frameworks. Aside from the legitimacy their governments gained from taking seats at the United Nations, or becoming
shareholders in the IMF and World Bank, the vast majority of the

available investment capital they needed to fund their own ambitious development projects was to be found in the West. The Soviet Union did attempt to create a rival communist economic bloc – the Council for Mutual Economic Assistance, or CMEA – but it was too ill-funded to offer much practical assistance to its member states. Western markets, by contrast, were rich and booming centres of demand, and once their economies got back on their feet, by the 1950s and 1960s, they had deep pockets once more. Many of the new governments emerging in the periphery, naturally rejecting the heritage of imperial domination, talked the talk of non-alignment. In practice, economic necessity left them firmly rooted in the Western camp.

In addition to the considerable influence that Western powers could exert on these new states individually – via financial aid, diplomatic influence, covert activities to support or oppose a government, and military pressure like port blockades – collectively, the Western powers could press developing world governments still more heavily to toe the line. Decisions in the United Nations General Assembly were taken on a one-country-one-vote principle, which favoured the plethora of new states, but votes in the Security Council, which could authorize the use of force, gave vetoes to its five permanent members: the US, the Soviet Union, France, China (represented until 1971 by the government in Taiwan) and Britain. Even more important, voting in the IMF and World Bank was conducted as in private corporations, with size of shareholding dictating weight of influence. The United States, as the single biggest contributor, had nearly a quarter of the votes and, between them, the Western powers controlled all the key decisions. They did not always agree – witness the Suez fiasco of 1956 – and the precise nature of relations with China or the Soviet Union varied from one Western country to the next. But on the key principles governing the global political economy – liberal trade, private property, market exchange – they found common cause.

Fundamentally, Bretton Woods institutionalized a global commercial order in which the net flow of global resources continued moving from the old imperial periphery of the global economy towards its Western imperial centre. The prevailing pattern of world development as it stood in 1945 meant that manufacturing initially remained heavily concentrated in the developed West. A liberal trade regime in manufactured goods thus enabled Western firms to dominate world markets in industrial goods, since any start-ups in the periphery would struggle to compete with the far more developed and better capitalized firms that held a tight grip on manufacturing expertise. In principle, developing countries could potentially build up their own economies by exporting agricultural and primary products back to the West. But because farmers constituted such an important political constituency in Western countries, their stock reinforced by recent experiences of hunger in World War II, the original GATT agreements did not liberalize trade in agricultural products to the same degree. Manufacturers in the periphery struggled to compete at home with Western imports, therefore, while its farmers faced considerable obstacles in expanding market share among Western consumers.

In the same period, the switch to the dollar as the unit of account steadily shifted the centre of the world economy from Britain to America. London remained one of the world's major banking centres, but its position at the apex of global finance was quickly ceded to New York.[10] In 1945 nearly nine-tenths of the world's foreign currency reserves were held in pounds sterling, and thus lodged with British banks (since only banks registered in Britain could provide account services in British currency). Over the next twenty-five years, that figure fell to less than a tenth, its place mostly taken by the US dollar, which by 1970 accounted for about three-quarters of the world's reserves.

As the reserves lodged in New York banks swelled, the pool of savings available to the US grew. All this money sitting in American bank accounts had to be put to work, since the governments holding them were being paid interest. Much of it was loaned to the US state – and, since its government didn't have to offer especially generous terms to attract sufficient funds, the overall effect was to keep interest rates low throughout the US banking system. Better yet, the American economy now enjoyed what amounted to an annual subsidy from the rest of the world. While in principle any government which held US dollars in its reserves could ask the American government to exchange them for the equivalent in gold from Fort Knox (at a fixed rate of $35 to the ounce), in practice, virtually all governments, even communist ones, seldom bothered: it was easier to let those dollars sit in US bank accounts rather than transport all that heavy gold back across the world to their own vaults – where, moreover, they would have to guard it. When governments traded among themselves, they would then just move their dollars across their respective US bank accounts, a much quicker and easier process than shipping physical gold.

This created a situation where any country which wanted to obtain US dollars needed to produce something it could sell, whereas the US could if necessary just print more money. It did so with glee, creating, in the quarter-century after the war, some three times more dollars than it had the gold reserves to back.[11] Essentially, the US Treasury gave other governments what amounted to IOUs, which they ended up hanging onto rather than cashing in. Over time, when it became apparent everyone was happy just to run up these virtual IOUs and swap them among themselves, the Treasury lost any need to earn them back, and could just pull them out of thin air. While other governments occasionally grumbled about this 'extraordinary privilege', nobody raised any serious objections. Peripheral governments couldn't do much about it – they usually needed hard currency more than anyone – while other Western governments ultimately benefited from the heavy post-war investment of American firms in Europe. In effect, what other Western countries gave to the US came right back to them. But because American investment in the periphery was so much more limited in the decades after the war, it was really peripheral countries that were losing out – effectively giving their products to America for free, which then got recirculated throughout the core of the world economy.

Apart from these particular advantages for the US, all the former imperial powers benefited from the one-way net flow of global wealth after 1945, while offloading the costs of colonial political administration onto the newly independent states, creating (for them) a win-win situation. The measures taken by many of the new states to augment their economic development then inadvertently intensified the flow. Opting for industrialization strategies to undercut the need for so many Western-manufactured imports in the longer term, as many of them did, required developing countries to buy Western technology, and to increase their exports of primary materials to cover the cost. This simultaneously swelled the market for Western exports and kept down the price of imported food and raw materials. Formal imperial political control had disappeared, but an imperial (or what was often called neo-colonial) economic system continued to function, materially benefiting the centre. As a result, the ratio of per-capita income between the 'West and the rest' rose from about thirty-to-one in 1950, to roughly double that at the end of the century. Formal decolonization had not remotely heralded the end of Western global domination. The practical operations of the Bretton Woods system not only redefined the Western Empire as a club of privileged nations headed by the United States, but allowed the latter to grow richer still post-war by continuing to reap the fruits of what remained a profoundly colonial trading and financial order.

The new-found political independence of the world's many new states was not a sham, far from it. Long-term economic and political development in the colonial era had eventually empowered much of the periphery to the point it was able to assert home rule and throw off direct imperial control. In some places, like Vietnam, Algeria and Indonesia, this required violent uprisings against imperial rule. But in most, it was done through negotiation, as the European empires recognized their time was up. And in the period after 1945, the new states created by this process began to enjoy real freedoms, with considerable latitude to determine their own affairs. But the implicit understanding was that they would do so within the rubric of a global economic system that was dominated by the Western powers, led by the United States. There was enough slack within the system for states to assert some of their own agendas without Western reprisals, as earlier Chilean governments found in the 1960s. But if they overstepped the bounds of their authority, threatening to break out of the Western system altogether, the weight of its continued hegemony would be exercised with decisive force, as Chilean President Salvador Allende and his followers discovered the hard way.

Allende had made the fatal mistake of overestimating the economic weight of the Soviet bloc, and the degree to which socialist links could act as a counterbalance to the Western Empire. In reality, the West dominated the world economy, accounting for the vast majority of its output, income and markets. Structural problems within the Russian economy along with its determination to maintain superpower-sized armed forces constantly sapped growth, and constrained the resources available to back diplomatic ambitions. Despite a facade of scientific achievement, symbolized by the Sputnik satellite and Yuri Gagarin's first-ever flight into space in 1961, the Soviet dependence upon exporting raw materials like oil and natural gas meant its economy more resembled that of a developing country in the amount of wealth it could generate, making it at best an apparent rival to the US and its allies. This 'Upper Volta with missiles' was so strapped for hard cash that supporting Cuba after the 1959 revolution drained most of its available resources, and even the Soviets needed US dollars to conduct overseas trade outside the CMEA bloc. This economic weakness, combined with the split between China and Russia which had resurfaced on the back of historic tensions again from the mid-1950s (resulting in a bout of actual if undeclared border warfare in 1969), effectively thwarted the formation of a global communist bloc to rival the West. Inevitably, therefore, when Allende looked to Moscow for support, he received polite words and little more.[12]

Like fourth-century Rome, the post-1945 West still largely managed to control the more robust clients in its inner periphery, while its own internal prosperity blossomed as never before. In neither case, however, did this happy situation represent an endpoint in the development of the respective imperial systems. The initial ambitions of assertive inner peripheries had been effectively contained, but much bigger challenges to continued imperial dominion would soon originate elsewhere.

PART TWO

PART TWO

5
Things Fall Apart

Imperial systems unravel for all kinds of reasons. Some get conquered. The Mongols swept out of the Eurasian steppe to end Song rule over China in fifty years of brutal campaigning. Some fall apart because of internal structural weakness. The Carolingian Empire – centred on France, western Germany and Italy – was basically a three-generation expansionary movement based on momentary military advantage, which collapsed as quickly as it had emerged. The end of the West Roman Empire fits into none of these simple categories.

Armed outsiders from beyond the frontiers – people the Romans customarily dismissed as 'barbarians' – had something to do with it. By AD 500 the vast majority of the territories of the old Western Empire had passed under the control of militarized groups of barbarians, who had crossed the frontier in the course of the previous century. Central and southern Britain was being parcelled out between Anglo-Saxon warband leaders from across the North Sea. Northern Gaul was ruled by Merovingian Frankish dynasts, and south-eastern Gaul belonged to Burgundian kings. Visigothic monarchs reigned over south-western Gaul and the bulk of the Iberian Peninsula, their Ostrogothic counterparts Italy, Sicily and the Dalmatian coast. The great city of Carthage and the richest provinces of North Africa were held by the Hasding dynasty, at the head of a coalition of Vandal and Alan warriors.

But many of these new kingdoms had not been created by simple conquest. The foreign military muscle behind two of them – the Visigothic and Vandal/Alan realms – was already established on West Roman soil by AD 410, but the last claimant to the West Roman imperial throne wouldn't be toppled for another seventy years. It was the West Roman government itself likewise that had originally settled the Burgundians on Roman soil in the 430s, while the Frankish and Ostrogothic kingdoms both came into existence only after the deposition of Romulus Augustulus – traditionally reckoned the last West Roman emperor – in September 476. The West Roman Empire ended up in the hands of barbarian dynasts, but this was no Mongol conquest.

The fall of the West, moreover, was only part one in a two-stage process of imperial unravelling. In AD 500 the eastern half of the Roman state – with its key revenue-producing centres in Asia Minor, Syria, Palestine, and Egypt – remained intact, and still exerted hegemony over much of the post-Roman West. The Burgundian kingdom (if admittedly for its own purposes) consistently acknowledged the notional superiority of the rulers of Constantinople in the early decades of the sixth century. And from the early 530s, the Eastern Emperor Justinian (527–65) was able to destroy the Vandal Alan and Ostrogothic kingdoms, and even, in the early 550s, annex a portion of the southern Iberian coastline. One hundred years further on, however, the eastern half of the Roman Empire had also fallen into eclipse.

The unravelling of the East Roman Empire began with twenty-five years of exhausting world war against its great Persian enemy at the start of the seventh century. The resulting bankruptcy of both empires then created a suitable context for large-scale expansion on the part of recently Islamicized Arabian forces in the middle decades of the century, which destroyed the Persian Empire entirely and robbed Constantinople of most of its richest provinces. In the 630s, Arab expansion swallowed up Syria and Palestine. Worse followed in the 650s, when Egypt was conquered, while the previously rich coastline of Asia Minor (home to some of the most famous cities of antiquity, such as Ephesus and Sardis) was turned into wasted battlefield: no longer a land of plenty but of fortifications and isolated villages. At this point, the real damage had been done, even if there were more conquests to come (North Africa would fall in the 690s). Because Constantinople itself managed to survive unconquered, the fact that the seventh century marked the effective end of the eastern half of the Roman Empire is sometimes overlooked. But Islamic conquest robbed the rulers of Constantinople of about three-quarters of their revenues, demoting the Empire from a true world power to a regional force at the eastern end of the Mediterranean. In reality, the new Byzantine Empire – named for Byzantium, as Constantinople had originally been known – was as much a successor state to the Roman Empire proper as any of the western kingdoms: an unwilling satellite state of the Islamic world, able to expand a little subsequently when this more powerful neighbour was in internal disarray, but condemned to diminish whenever Islamic unity was restored.

Played out over two and a half centuries, the full unravelling of the Roman imperial system – as even a brief outline makes clear – involved complex interactions between a number of disparate factors. This is why so many different explanations have been offered over the years for Rome's fall. It is also self-evidently the case that the modern Western Empire has not fallen, will not fall anytime soon, and in fact need never fall in the same way as its ancient predecessor. Rome's economy was fundamentally steady-state and agrarian, which turned wealth and power at the highest level into a zero-sum game. For there to be political winners, there had to be losers. Power was based on the control of a more or less stable stock of agrarian assets, and if the system started to face serious challenges, you couldn't just generate vast amounts of new wealth to ride out the problems by enlarging the number of winners. This again is much less obviously the case for its modern Western counterpart whose history, as we have been examining, has been characterized by centuries of exponential economic growth.

Nonetheless, there is every reason to suppose that the modern West's imperial life cycle has at the very least reached a major tipping point. In what is clearly far more than a blip, its share of global GDP has fallen by more than a quarter in less than two decades. Against this backdrop, sustained comparison with the unravelling of the Roman system, despite many differences in context and precise detail, continues – we would argue – to possess great explanatory power. But from this point on, the comparison has to proceed a little differently, since Rome's fall is complete, and the future history of the West contains many unknowns (of both the known and unknown variety). It is not possible, therefore, to continue with a simple side-by-side comparison. Nonetheless, a set of unfolding patterns is already clear enough in the modern world to make it possible to use Roman history to show, first, that the West is currently experiencing only the beginnings of what will be an unfolding and potentially even existential crisis, and, second, that this crisis is revolving around the same key components which undermined its ancient Roman counterpart. The best place to begin the analysis is with a brief survey of the key factors at the heart of Rome's collapse.

THE RISE OF THE NORTH

In the summer of 773, Charlemagne crossed the Alps, and trapped the Lombard king Desiderius inside his capital at Pavia. The siege lasted into the following summer, but Desiderius was eventually despatched to a convenient monastery and Charlemagne, already king of the Franks and quickly crowned king of Italy, accepted the submission of the Lombard nobility. This was the beginning of the Carolingian Empire. Though it failed to develop anything like the durability of its Roman predecessor, the rise of a new centre of European imperial power in what had been part of Rome's periphery illustrates one of the key factors behind Roman imperial collapse.

Charlemagne's economic and demographic power base lay in the north-east of the Frankish kingdom, spanning both sides of the old Roman frontier and encompassing territory in what is now north-western France, Benelux, and western Germany. At the start of the first millennium, the populations of these regions had either been too weak to resist Roman conquest, or so underdeveloped that the Romans had decided it was not worth incorporating them formally into the Empire (p. 39). In stark contrast, Charlemagne was able to use the now much-expanded demographic and economic resources of this region to conquer significant tracts of Mediterranean real estate. Nor, although the Carolingian Empire itself failed to last, was this a one-off. The tenth-century Ottonian successors of the Carolingians, whose power base lay still further east between the Rhine and the Elbe, used northern resources to conquer most of Italy again in the tenth century. In the course of the first millennium, the whole geopolitical balance of power on which the Roman Empire had been based – using Mediterranean wealth and manpower to conquer in the north – was inverted, and the new pattern which made Charlemagne possible has held broadly good ever since. Northern Europe has consistently been home to larger populations and bigger economies, and hence tended to dominate the Mediterranean south.

The explanation for this decisive shift in the European balance of power is straightforward. Mediterranean Europe is home to highly fertile, lighter soils, which were easier to exploit in antiquity without expensive, complicated agricultural equipment. Northern Europe offers incomparably greater resources overall, but the technological problems involved in fully exploiting both its wetter and heavier soils and its extensive marine resources are more complex. By the time of Charlemagne, the *carruca*, the classic northern heavy plough – a massive iron ploughshare mounted on a four-wheeled wagon pulled by teams of up to eight animals – was already coming into use, northern productivity was on the rise, and the balance of European economic and demographic power had begun to shift.

This long-term strategic revolution must be reckoned one of the biggest stories of the whole first millennium. Though the Roman Empire was not responsible for all of it, Charlemagne's Empire does represent the climax of long-term processes of development which had been kick-started by four centuries of interaction between the Roman centre and its European peripheries. In the inner periphery, agricultural productivity and population densities had already increased significantly during the Roman period (Chapter 3) and kept moving subsequently, until, by the eighth century, they had undermined the basic power distribution upon which Rome's Mediterranean-based domination of western Eurasia had rested.

Some of the political consequences of this process of long-term development were already visible by the third century, generating the more powerful 'barbarian' confederations which expanded into former imperial territory in northern Britain, between the upper Rhine and Danube, and in Transylvania (p. 60). Political entities based in the inner periphery played a still larger role in the unravelling of the West Roman system in the fifth century. The Anglo-Saxon warbands which prospered so mightily in former Roman Britain originated in Rome's north-western inner periphery, as did the Frankish kingdom which Charlemagne eventually turned into an Empire. Even though this ongoing transformation had not reached maturity by the fifth century, it had still gone far enough to help swing the balance of power against the continued existence of Rome's Mediterranean-based imperial power.

SUPERPOWER COMPETITION

A rock carving at Bishapur in modern Iran portrays the grovelling submission of the captive Roman Emperor Valerian to the Persian Shah-in-shah (king of kings), Shapur I (240–72). In Shapur's own words, inscribed in three languages around the great Zoroastrian fire temple at Naqs-i Rustam:

> When I was first established over the dominion of the nations, the Cae-sar Gordian raised an army and marched against us. Gordian was destroyed and the Roman army annihilated. The Romans proclaimed Philip Caesar. And Philip came to sue for peace, and for their lives he paid a ransom of 500,000 denarii and became tributary to us. And the Caesar lied again and did injustice to Armenia. We marched against the Roman Empire and annihilated a Roman army of 60,000 men at Bar-balissos. In the campaign [we took] thirty-seven cities. In the third contest ... Caesar Valerian came upon us. There was with him a force of 70,000 men ... We took him prisoner with our own hands, as well as all the other commanders of the army. On this campaign, we con-quered thirty-six cities.

Mobilizing the human and economic resources of what is now Iraq and Iran more effectively than its Arsacid predecessors, the Sasanian dynasty – to which Shapur belonged – built up its control of the Near East across the third century, and was already winning victories over Rome in the time of Shapur's father Ardashir (224–40). What had destroyed Arsacid control was a further bout of Roman expansion at the end of the second century, which had seen Septimius Severus cre-ate two new provinces in what is now Syria and Iraq and advance the imperial frontier far to the south and east. This defeat fatally undermined the Arsacids – who had run the Persian world since 247 BC – and allowed the Sasanians to triumph. The emergence of Sasanian Persia as a peer superpower competitor to Rome must be seen, therefore, like the emergence of new confederations in the European peripheries, as a dynamic, regional-level response to Roman imperialism. In the Persian case, however, this was more of a military and political reorganization within a world which had been home to complex civilizations since the fourth millennium BC, rather than the kind of long-term demographic and economic expansion which underpinned the Carolingian Empire.

War with Persia would eventually play a catalytic role in Eastern Rome's loss of superpower status in the seventh century, but it was already a factor in the fifth-century Western collapse. From the third century onwards Persia's reassertion of superpower status consistently stretched the Roman Empire much more profoundly than the contemporary problems in the European inner periphery which led to Alamanni's occupation of the upper Rhine or the loss of Transylvanian Dacia. None of the new European confederations was capable of winning victories on the scale of Shapur's destruction of three full-scale Roman field armies,[13] a catastrophic sequence of defeat which forced a fundamental restructuring of the Roman system in response. By conservative estimates, Rome's army had to expand in the course of the third century by at least 50 per cent (some argue it doubled). And because the Roman state spent around 75 per cent of its limited tax revenues on the military, such a vast expansion in troop numbers posed a huge fiscal headache, demanding the total tax-take increase by over a third. When you compare how difficult modern politicians find it to increase spending on health by even 1 or 2 per cent, when health is only about 8 per cent of total government spending, the scale of the systemic problem posed by Persia is apparent.

Grabbing what remained of the old city revenues (the shift which eventually pushed provincial elites like Ausonius towards imperial careers: Chapter 2) was one immediate response, as was the progressive devaluation of the silver denarius. This was the currency in which legionaries had always been paid, and a progressive series of devaluations underlay the famous hyper-inflation of the second half of the third century (p. 13). Due to the massive increase in troop numbers, there was no longer enough metal in the Empire to mint pure silver coins in sufficient quantities. When these short-term fixes proved ineffective, the longer-term structural response was a tighter tax regime and a revolution in army pay, which shifted from silver coin to a mix of regular distributions of materials in kind (of food, equipment and other essentials), and occasional payments in pure gold. By the last decades of the third century, these measures had produced reasonably paid Roman soldiers in sufficient numbers to counter more grandiose Sasanian ambitions.

Revamped, reinforced Roman armies began to win significant victories in the east again by the 290s, but Sasanian Persia remained a superpower: a permanent peer competitor to the Roman imperial system, a situation with which it had never previously been faced. This meant that a huge proportion of the available military and fiscal resources of the Empire had always to be pointed in a Persian direction: somewhere between a quarter and a third of Rome's entire military establishment. If any significant element of these forces was shifted elsewhere to deal with other problems, Persia's rulers usually took the opportunity to exploit the situation.

Still worse, the rise of Persia generated important structural effects which further hampered the working of the Roman system. Because of the slowness of communications, the huge forces countering Persian aggression in the east required close political scrutiny, or their commander was always likely to make a bid for the purple. This was an important lesson learned the hard way on multiple occasions in the third century. But an emperor who was on hand to supervise the eastern front was too far away to control the other main centre of Roman military force on the Rhine frontier, and to distribute well-directed patronage to the Western elites whose active participation made the imperial system work. Hence, from the later third century onwards, imperial power was generally divided between at least two and occasionally more emperors.

This outcome was unavoidable, as several failed attempts at sole rule in the late Roman period showed, but dividing imperial power materially affected the smooth operation of the system. No one ruler commanded all its resources, and there were regular bouts of tension between co-emperors – even those from the same family – which periodically went as far as civil war. Across most of the fourth century, more Roman soldiers died fighting in these periodic civil wars than in battle against European barbarians (though continued conflict with Persia killed them in still greater numbers). Overall, therefore, the rise of Persia both reduced the amount of structural flex – in terms of economic and demographic resources – left within the Roman system for dealing with further problems, and made it more difficult to mobilize these resources in a unified way. The significance of both developments would soon become clear when entirely new threats appeared in the later fourth century.

EXOGENOUS SHOCK

Late in the summer of 376 two large groups of barbarian Goths appeared on the banks of the Danube. They were requesting asylum in return for a military alliance. One group, the Tervingi, were admitted, but the Greuthungi were rejected: attempted damage limitation. Fully engaged the best part of a thousand kilometres to the east in another major confrontation with Persia, it was two years before the current ruler of the eastern Empire, Valens, could extract his field armies from the east, and for the moment he had nothing like enough troops to exclude both Gothic groups from Roman territory.

As it turned out, Valens' attempt to divide and rule came to nothing. The Tervingi, once inside the frontier, grew restive in the face of food shortages. The problem was aggravated by the Romans – clearly foreseeing the potential for trouble and acting accordingly – having moved available supplies into defended bases which the Goths could not easily capture. The local Roman commander then panicked, launching an abortive attack on the Goths' leaders whom he'd invited to dinner: the final straw which pushed the Tervingi into rebellion. Their leaders had anyway been maintaining contact with the excluded Greuthungi, who now crossed into Roman territory as well, so that by the start of 377 Valens was facing a united Gothic revolt. Two campaigning seasons later, Valens had bought peace from Persia, and was finally in a position to move his field army westwards. The emperor advanced into the Balkans with one force, while the Western Emperor, his nephew Gratian, advanced east to meet him with another. But Gratian was delayed and Valens grew impatient, eventually sprinting north to Hadrianople: modern Edirne close to the Turkish/Bulgarian border. Scouts had reported that the two Gothic forces had split up to spread the burden of finding supplies, and Valens hoped to ambush just the Tervingi. The report was mistaken. On the morning of 9 August 378 the East Roman field army rushed into action, but was itself ambushed. The Greuthungi were also present. In the resulting massacre, the emperor and two-thirds of his army were slaughtered. This sequence of events looks like a classic example of barbarian invasion, which in one sense it was, but there is another much more important dimension to the story.

The Goths had not wanted to invade the Roman Empire. As with modern examples of mass migration, it's important never to underestimate the enormous dangers and costs involved in upping sticks and heading to pastures new. The Goths who arrived on the Danube in 376 had been part of the wider imperial system, occupying lands in the inner periphery, for the best part of a hundred years, but were set in motion by exogenous shock: the predatory intrusion into the Goths' territories of nomadic Huns from the great Eurasian steppe. The Greuthungi were in the front line against the Huns and resisted for some time, but eventually concluded that life in what is now Ukraine had become untenable. They began an organized withdrawal westwards, which in turn destabilized their neighbours, the Tervingi. Why the Huns themselves were on the move is not convincingly explained in the ancient sources, but recently analysed ice-core samples suggest that unusual weather patterns in the early 370s had generated a period of sustained drought on the steppe. This would have put great pressure on nomadic groups like the Huns who relied on these always marginal grazing lands to support their herds.[14] The real cause of Valens' Gothic problem, therefore, lay not in the inner imperial periphery but in a human tsunami unleashed in the outer periphery and beyond, which – on further reflection – makes perfect sense.

Empires not only unintentionally set loose political transformation among their immediate neighbours, but populations less directly involved in the imperial system also actively respond to the dangers and opportunities presented by the emergence of an adjacent super-power. In the Roman case, this periodically took the form of groups originally from the outer European periphery – the world of Rome's amber and slave traders closer to the Baltic, rather than its agricultural suppliers living close to the actual frontier – who reorganized themselves on occasion to seize control of new lands in the immediate fringes of Empire. Much, for instance, of the European action behind Rome's third-century crisis – which as we saw in the last chapter ended up with some limited erosion of direct imperial control beyond the Rhine and Danube frontier lines – had its roots in precisely this pattern. Both the Goths and Alamanni who played a starring role in the action had begun the third century in Rome's outer periphery, organizing themselves in the course of it to seize profitable new positions much closer to the Empire's frontier.[15] What always attracted the attention of Roman commentators were the knock-on effects of these movements in terms of cross-border raiding, but the deeper roots of the third-century crisis lay much further afield. Inner peripheral groups were generally wealthier and better organized, but they were also more under the imperial thumb, making it much less likely that they would be the prime source of serious instability within the system as a whole.

The same dynamic played a major role in the eventual unravelling of the western half of the Roman imperial system in the later fourth and fifth centuries. In this case, the events of the later 370s, which saw not merely the Goths but several other Lower Danubian groups take to the road, represented only the first instalment of a much larger crisis generated by Hunnic expansion from the western steppe into eastern and then central Europe. A generation after 376, large numbers of Huns moved from Europe's eastern fringes in Ukraine to the Great Hungarian Plain on the western side of the Carpathian mountains; it is unclear if this was from necessity or ambition. This prompted a second bout of intense instability, now affecting the central European Middle Danubian sector of Rome's European frontiers. In 405 one large mixed force left this region, moving south through what is now Austria to burst into Italy under the leadership of a Gothic king called Radagaisus. They were followed onto Roman territory at the end of 406 by an extremely large if loose alliance of various groups from the same Middle Danubian region, with four major components: nomadic Alans under several kings, two separate groups of Vandals, and an assorted body of Suevi. The Alans had been the Goths' eastern neighbours in Ukraine in the 370s, but had been displaced westwards in the interim; the other participants were all long-standing residents of central Europe. This second force chose a different route onto Roman territory, breaking over the Upper Rhine into Gaul on the last day of 406, but both were probably on the move to escape the Huns, who were securely established in their old domains on the Great Hungarian Plain by around 410.[16]

The crisis of the late fourth and early fifth centuries, like that of the third, was fundamentally a dose of exogenous shock, therefore, with its roots in the outer periphery of the Roman system and beyond, even if it was inner peripheral groups who were largely pushed into direct conflict with the Empire. And whereas the Roman system had had enough residual flex to deal with earlier crises of this kind with only small-scale losses of territory, the knock-on effects of Hunnic expansion caused much greater problems altogether. Not only, by this stage, had the rise of Persia eroded much of the spare capacity available to Rome's rulers, but, once so many different barbarian groups had been displaced onto Roman soil, the system itself began to suffer still further disruption on an entirely unprecedented scale.

The initial response of Roman emperors to the arrival of large numbers of uninvited outsiders, many of them armed and well-organized, was – unsurprisingly – hostility and suspicion. As with Valens and the Goths of 376, this usually led to military confrontation, and Rome's efforts often enjoyed substantial success. Although the Goths of 376 eventually won a stunning victory at Hadrianople, they had suffered major losses in the run-up, which saw the wholesale elimination of dispersed sub-groups sent out on foraging expeditions. The battle at Hadrianople also cost them heavily, as did the four further years of indecisive warfare which preceded the peace deal they eventually negotiated with the Empire in October 382. In the next generation, Radagaisus' invasion of Italy was quickly neutralized in the summer of 406. Many of his elite military followers were won over by a deal with the Empire which saw them drafted into the

Roman army, at the expense of both their leader – who was executed outside Florence – and many of their less fortunate, lower-status colleagues. So many of the latter were sold into slavery that the bottom fell out of the Italian slave market. An effective response to the Vandals and Alans who crossed the Rhine at the end of 406 took longer to organize, by which time the members of the alliance had moved into Roman Spain and divided up its provinces between them. In the mid-410s, however, a series of punishing Roman counter-attacks destroyed the independence of the various Alanic groups and also one of the two Vandal groups – the Silings – completely eliminating their royal dynasties in battle or by capture.

Substantial as they were, none of these military successes was enough to neutralize the overall problem posed by the displaced 'barbarian' groupings, and, in one important sense, made it worse. Faced with periodically effective Roman counterattack, the survivors of the initial clashes reorganized themselves into larger and more coherent confederations: exactly what they needed to do to survive in the face of Roman military power. The original distinction between Tervingi and Greuthungi disappeared on Roman soil. From the 380s onwards the Romans were facing one united Gothic force (commonly called the Visigoths) which, under the leadership of a king called Alaric (c. 395–411), moved definitively westwards in 408, seeking to exploit the chaos that the combined invasions of Radagaisus and the Rhine confederation had generated. Once there, Alaric recruited many of the survivors of Radagaisus' invasion: both those elite elements originally drafted into the Roman army (whose families had since been massacred in anti-barbarian pogroms) and those sold into slavery. The Alanic and Siling Vandal survivors of the defeats of 416–18 likewise united themselves behind the other Vandal royal dynasty – the Hasdings – in southern Spain, again forming a larger, more consolidated coalition. In 422 this new confederation won its own battle of Hadrianople outside the walls of Cordoba in southern Spain, defeating the Roman forces primarily because a Visigothic contingent serving with the Roman army changed sides – by pre-arrangement – at the crucial moment. By the early 420s, therefore, the overall effect of the massive dose of exogenous shock administered by the Huns had become clear. Two enlarged, newly consolidated confederations, composed primarily of recent immigrants from the inner periphery, had established themselves on West Roman soil.

Over the next two political generations, these confederations went on to establish two of the main successor states to the western half of the Roman Empire, and this was no accident; their whole existence undermined the integrity of the imperial system. Most immediately, their victories killed off large numbers of Roman soldiers. Hadrianople cost the East Roman army at least 10,000 dead out of a total force of 15,000 men (more extravagant estimates make that 20,000 out of 30,000).[17] A West Roman military listing, dating just after the Vandals' signature victory of 422, likewise underlines the scale of loss inflicted upon the West Roman army up to that point. As much as two-thirds of the West Roman field army, as it had stood in 395, had been destroyed in the intervening quarter-century of campaigning.

Well-trained Roman troops were expensive, but even entire units could be replaced in time, so long as the necessary resources were available. And in the east they were. After Hadrianople, the Goths never got anywhere near the Eastern Empire's crucial tax-generating, heavily populated regions in Egypt, Asia Minor and the Fertile Crescent. The problem facing the West in its final decades, after the Visigothic and Vandal-Alan confederations had established themselves on its territories by the early 420s, was much more profound.

The existence of two large foreign confederations on Roman soil directly threatened the Empire's key military–fiscal axis. Areas caught up in their periodic conflicts with the Roman state suffered substantial damage to fields, crops and livestock. A full decade after they had been subject to Visigothic occupation (408–10), central and southern Italian provinces were still receiving a 90 per cent tax reduction, seemingly a standard level of fiscal mitigation offered to farming regions affected by serious fighting. Comparative evidence suggests that it probably took about twenty years to make good any damage to livestock, equipment and buildings, and to pay off the debts and interest incurred in taking out the necessary loans for doing so. Other areas were permanently removed from the Roman state's tax base altogether, if after the fighting they were occupied by either of the confederations. Hence, by the early 420s, most of Spain had not been producing tax revenue for the best part of decade, parts of southern

Gaul and central/southern Italy had suffered in extensive warfare, and Britain had dropped out of the imperial system altogether (for reasons which we'll turn to next). This adds up to substantial losses in tax revenue (25 per cent or more) for the Western Empire, and the effects show up in that same military listing of the early 420s. Whereas the East eventually made good its losses at Hadrianople, the Western Empire could no longer afford to. It replaced the vast majority of its field army losses in the period 405–22 simply by upgrading existing frontier garrison troops on paper to field-army status, not by 'proper' (i.e. expensive) new recruitment.[18]

There was worse to come. In 432 the Vandal-Alan coalition crossed the Straits of Gibraltar, and, seven years later, seized the jewel in the West Roman imperial crown: its richest revenue-producing territories in what is now Algeria and Tunisia. The imperial centre had already been struggling to maintain its armies in the 420s and this loss plunged it further into crisis, threatening a vicious spiral where declining revenues would mean fewer troops and still more opportunities for the barbarian confederations to seize further Roman territory. The exogenous shock generated by the Huns thus threatened the fundamental fiscal-military axis on which the entire imperial system had been constructed.

INTERNAL DIVISION

In January 414 a wedding of unusual splendour was held in the old Roman city of Narbonne in southern Gaul. The sister of the Western Emperor Honorius, Galla Placidia, was getting married: no expense spared. The Roman senator Priscus Attalus – a younger contemporary of our old friend Symmachus whose metropolitan condescension got him into trouble on his trip to the north-west frontier (p. 33) – was drafted in to decorate the event with appropriate classical verse: the epithalamium which traditionally serenaded a bride to her wedding chamber. Unfortunately, Attalus' poem hasn't survived. Its contents would make fascinating reading. It was not just that Narbonne – despite its still wonderful Roman remains – was an unusual setting for an imperial wedding: the groom was also a Visigothic king. Galla had been captured when the Visigoths sacked Rome four years earlier, and was now marrying Alaric's brother-in-law Athaulf.

This extraordinary wedding formed part of a calculated policy of semi-rapprochement in the aftermath of that attack. Even the sack of Rome was not quite what it seemed. Alaric's forces had been sitting outside the city for eighteen months, and could have entered the city at any point. They had refrained, because Alaric was threatening the city as a bargaining chip to force Galla's brother Honorius into a long-term political deal. Alaric let his forces loose only when it became clear that the emperor, led by his current advisors, was unwilling to negotiate in good faith. As far as both Alaric and Athaulf were concerned, the Western Empire was a permanent feature of the political landscape and both wanted to embed the Goths within its structures on the best possible terms. Athaulf's marriage would add his Gothic followers to the (declining) muster of field army troops of the Western Empire, ensuring them a regular income – but they would remain under his autonomous leadership, making him a major figure at the imperial court. At the same time, like Alaric, he never shied away from conflict with the Empire in pursuit of his highly ambitious political agendas. Priscus Attalus had already been declared emperor with Gothic support once by Alaric outside Rome, and was raised to the purple a second time by Athaulf in Gaul. The king's marriage to Galla Placidia was also completed without her brother's permission, and, when the union quickly produced a son, he was given the highly significant name of Theodosius. The original Theodosius (the first) was Honorius' imperial father who reigned from 379 to 395, founder of the imperial dynasty that now ruled in both east and west, and Honorius himself was childless. This was a baby, despite his Gothic father, with serious claims to the Western throne.

In the end, Athaulf's purple ambitions were misjudged. Theodosius died in infancy, and when Honorius finally found himself more capable advisors, it quickly became clear that enough force still remained in the Western Empire to corral the new Visigothic confederation. After two years of well-placed economic blockades, the Goths were starved into accepting a settlement in south-western Gaul which placed them far from the Italian centre of Western politics. Athaulf himself had already been assassinated by internal Gothic rivals when it became clear that his strategy of rapprochement was failing. It was also part of the emerging new deal that Galla Placidia was returned to her brother, and Gothic forces were committed to campaigning against the Vandals and Alans in Spain (p. 9).

But if it failed in its grandest designs, the reign of Athaulf revealed the first inklings of a major fault line within the imperial landowning elite which would go on to play an important role in the story of West Roman collapse. Galla herself, perhaps attracted by the prospect of an unexpectedly exciting future as dowager empress, seems to have been a voluntary partner in her marriage. Her lot in life may otherwise have been a closeted retirement in the city of Rome, designed to prevent anyone from using her to generate potential heirs as their own pathway to power at court. Priscus Attalus, too, is nothing out of the ordinary; history throws up many examples of politicians desperate enough for power to seek it under any circumstances, no matter how ignominious. What's so much more striking about Athaulf's manoeuvring, however, is that various members of the provincial landowning elite were willing to serve Attalus' usurping regime in both its Italian and later Gallic episodes, even though it was completely dependent upon Gothic rather than Roman imperial military manpower.

There are a few hints that the new barbarian confederations – Alaric's Visigoths and the Vandal-Alans – may have recruited some of their new manpower from disaffected elements among the Roman lower classes, but the evidence is not conclusive. Much better documented, and much more important in political terms, was this willingness of some members of the Roman landowning elite – descendants of the likes of Ausonius – to throw in their lot with the barbarian confederations now in their midst. Athaulf recruited some Gallo-Roman supporters in the 410s, the Vandals took some high-status Hispano-Romans with them to North Africa in the 430s, and Romano-British provincials recruited Anglo-Saxon mercenaries from across the North Sea (mainly from areas that are now in Denmark and northern Germany) in the 420s and 430s to help defend their assets against raiders from Scotland and Ireland.

The phenomenon is best documented, however, in the political generation active after about 450. From this era we have a letter collection penned by one provincial aristocrat from the Auvergne: a man named Sidonius Apollinaris. Sidonius' correspondence catalogues a range of different collaborations between his Gallic landowning peers and neighbouring Visigothic and Burgundian kings.[19] Sidonius himself and some of his closest allies were happy to ally with either, so long as their leaderships – following the lead of Alaric and Athaulf – were deploying their military power to support the continued existence of some kind of Western Empire. In 457, for instance, Sidonius penned a striking portrait of the Visigothic ruler Theodoric II, presenting the king not as a barbarian monarch, but as a civilized Roman ruler at a moment when Theodoric was supporting the (temporarily successful) bid of Sidonius' father-in-law to seize the vacant Western throne. It emphasized that the king banned from his court over-indulgence in wine and food: ever a barbarian characteristic as far as Romans were concerned. In the later 460s and early 470s, however, Sidonius' close circle raised private armies against the incursions of Theodoric's younger brother Euric, to try to remain part of a now shrinking imperial core. But if there were clear limits to Sidonius' willingness to collaborate, other members of the Gallic elite took a different view. By the same date some of his other acquaintances were already prominent advisors to Visigothic and Burgundian kings and positively encouraging them to expand the borders of their emergent kingdoms.[20]

The willingness of local Roman elites to throw in their lot with leaders other than crowned emperors reflects – at first sight counter-intuitively – the increasing political maturity of late Roman provincial society. The same processes of development which brought men like Ausonius to the fore had simultaneously created groupings of provincial aristocrats capable of formulating and pursuing their own political agendas. Already in the third century, when the rise of Persia made a succession of emperors focus so much attention on the east, this had manifested itself in a willingness among Western, particularly Gallic elites to back usurping emperors who would prioritize their needs. And so again in the fifth century: when the West Roman political centre was perceived by them as failing, at least some West Roman provincial landowners were willing to contemplate radical alternative solutions.

THE FALL OF ROME

Different scholars arrange these contributory factors in different orders of importance, but for present purposes the exact weighting to be placed on each of the contributory factors is insignificant. The more fundamental point is that all serious modern discussions of Rome's fall essentially focus on this same list of factors.

As the system unravelled, the Roman Empire found itself caught in a downward spiral. Superpower rivalry and the self-assertion of a developing inner periphery combined with a substantial flow of migration from the outer periphery and beyond to impose extra stress upon the system, and all this intertwined with sometimes bitter internal political division on a series of levels. Each of these different components had its own specific lines of cause and effect, but nearly all of them (the lack of rainfall on the Eurasian steppe apart) were epiphenomena of broader transformations set in motion by the workings of the Roman imperial system. The Persian Empire's restoration from the third century was a direct response to Roman territorial expansion. The new Vandal-Alan and Visigothic coalitions were products both of the long-term economic and political transformations that four hundred years of Roman imperial dominion had worked on its neighbours and an immediate response to Roman military counter-attack. It was, likewise, the new-found wealth of the inner periphery which attracted groups from the outer periphery and beyond to push these neighbours onto Roman soil, and expose fault lines between east and west, and central and local power within the Roman system.

However you reconstruct the precise interconnections of cause and effect, therefore, a relatively simple thread runs through the narrative of Roman imperial collapse. As the rising periphery's ability to compete with the Empire grew, the Empire had to direct more of its resources both to negating the Persian threat and to preserving its European frontiers. This increased its vulnerability to exogenous shocks from outside the system, which it might easily have withstood at earlier stages of its development. The rise of a hostile peer-competitor in Persia also enforced a problematic division of the imperial office, which, along with the sudden appearance of the Huns from the east, eventually tipped the balance against the Empire. At this point, the imperial centre was no longer able to protect the interests of some key political constituencies, who shifted their allegiances elsewhere.

The chapters which follow will argue that the developing crisis of the modern Western Empire combines exactly the same moving parts: exogenous shock (including large-scale migration) originating in the outer periphery and beyond, an assertive inner periphery, peer superpower competition, and growing internal political stress. Exactly how, and to what extent, the modern system will – like its Roman predecessor – unravel over the coming few decades depends of course on the cumulative effect of the policy choices made in response to each of these problems. But not only can Roman history allow us to identify all of these problems as consequences of the workings of the imperial system, it can also help us to think more analytically both about the kinds of responses currently being made, and their likely outcomes over the longer term. So far, modern political discourse has mobilized the Roman past to discuss just one of these problems – migration – so our analysis will begin by taking a much closer look at this most highly charged topic of current debate.

6

Barbarian Invasions

The one part of the former Western Empire which saw the complete collapse of Roman civilization was Britain. Latin, villas, education, written law, Christianity: all the characteristic trappings of classical culture disappeared north of the Channel, along with every sign of complex economic exchange. In the 1980s there was hope that new, more sophisticated archaeological methods might bring to light some substantial post-Roman urbanism which had previously been missed. Forty years on, all that has emerged is one renovated water pipe in St Albans in Hertfordshire and a few slightly unconvincing postholes at Wroxeter in Shropshire. Some ninth-century Anglo-Saxon pottery found under the tiles of the collapsed roof of the Roman legionary headquarters in York subsequently proved to be the handiwork of burrowing rabbits, not a sign that its Praetorium was still standing in AD 800. Along with the vanishing of towns proper in the few decades after 400 went craft and manufacture – specialist pottery industries were replaced with localized handmade production – and coins fell completely out of use. Things became so desperate there was even a market in reworked broken glass.

From the mid-nineteenth century, academics concentrated on one primary explanation for all the destruction: the arrival of primitive Anglo-Saxon immigrants. It had long been realized that English, despite Latinate add-ons mostly transmitted by the Normans, was fundamentally a Germanic language. But in this period Victorian philologists also worked out that pretty much every English place name, down to the smallest stream or bump in the landscape, had Anglo-Saxon, not Celtic or Latin, roots. When the first flowering of scientific archaeology in the latter part of that century correctly identified the arrival north of the Channel of a new material culture, broadly dated to the fifth century, whose roots evidently lay in non-Roman northern Europe, the conclusion seemed obvious. Roman civilization in Britain had been undone by the arrival of a mass of Anglo-Saxons from across the North Sea, who drove those of the Romanized Celts they hadn't killed into Wales, Cornwall and Brittany.

Post-Roman Britain was the worst-case scenario, but by the end of the fifth century an apparently similar script was unfolding across the vast majority of the former Western Empire. Everywhere, imperial Roman rule was being replaced by immigrant royal dynasties, inaugurating a period infamous for supposed cultural and economic decline on a vast scale: the so-called 'Dark Ages'.

THE FIRST BREXIT

Recent work in archaeology and genetics has forced a major rethink of the thesis that a mass of Anglo-Saxon migrants demographically overwhelmed Roman civilization. Slightly more migrants (in percentage terms) probably did come to Britain in the fifth century than to other parts of the former Roman west, but numbers weren't the real issue. Up to the 1950s, Roman civilization north of the Channel was viewed as a thin veneer on top of a still substantially wild landscape, with only a limited population. One distinguished historian of the era characterized the Anglo-Saxon take-over as less a struggle between immigrant and native than a story of 'man against tree', making it much easier to think of a small, disparate indigenous population being physically driven to the geographical margins by incoming Anglo-Saxons. The last two generations of scholarship have made it clear, however, that this rested on a fundamental misapprehension. With the intensification of archaeological survey work, the number of known Roman-era settlements has increased exponentially, to the point that the population of late-Roman Britain is now estimated to have been at the same kind of maximum level for a pre-modern era – four million plus – that would only be achieved again on the eve of the Black Death in the early fourteenth century: a thousand years later. The idea that this many people could have been driven into Britain's western fringes is ludicrous.

Along with increased survey work have come extraordinary advances in genetic analysis. Some of it has been misinterpreted and misapplied in ultra-nationalist circles to support a contention that there was (and is) a genetically identifiable English population, whose position is now being threatened by excessive migration. It is the case that one particular Y chromosome mutation is widely distributed among modern English males: 40–50 per cent of those descended from male ancestors who were native to England before the Industrial Revolution put Britain and Europe's population on the move. This mutation probably did originate among a north European population cluster somewhere on the other side of the North Sea. But to conclude that this means the Anglo-Saxon period saw a 50 per cent population replacement by immigrants is deeply flawed. You cannot date when the mutation first appeared, so it may well have been shared among male Celts, Anglo-Saxons and Vikings: all of whom were involved in different migration flows into Britain from northern continental Europe. And even if it could be securely identified as somehow particularly Anglo-Saxon (there is no prospect that it can), what has been measured is its distribution among modern English males of the twenty-first century, not its prevalence in the period of Anglo-Saxon migration. Anglo-Saxon migrants became the dominant landholding group in southern Britain in the fifth and sixth centuries, which means that they had considerable advantages in access to food and other forms of wealth. As subsequent modelling has shown, you only need to allocate these migrants a small advantage in passing on their genes – which their social position would certainly have given them – and the current 40–50 per cent distribution of the mutation can be easily and quickly achieved from an immigrant male population which originally numbered only between 5 and 10 per cent of the total. This would still represent a larger immigrant percentage than anywhere else on the continent (Goths and Vandals are unlikely to have numbered more than a per cent of the total population of the lands they acquired closer to the Mediterranean), but doesn't fundamentally change the picture. However you look at it, the fifth and sixth centuries saw relatively few Anglo-Saxon migrants interacting with an indigenous mass of Roman Britons, and the biggest genetic advance of all has demonstrated that there is no such thing as genetically definable English (or French, or Norwegians for that matter).[21]

The real explanation for the extent of Roman civilization's collapse in Britain lies not in the scale of migration which unfolded north of the Channel, but in the scale of negotiation. On the continent, especially after the defeat of Constantinople's Vandal expedition of 468, large tracts of Roman territory began to fall at a stroke under the control of the new, much-enlarged confederations. As a result, Visigothic, Vandal, and – later – Frankish and Ostrogothic kings found themselves negotiating with large numbers of the sitting Roman landowning elite in their newly acquired territories. And, en masse, this elite had some serious bargaining chips to offer: ready-made practical social control over a mass of peasant producers, ideologies of power, and administrative capacity, not least to raise tax revenues, which could all help stabilize the new states hastily being improvised. In these circumstances, all the emerging continental monarchies happily negotiated versions of a similar deal, with the result that, in many areas south of the Channel, the post-imperial social order still encompassed numerous Roman landowners, who between them preserved substantial elements of Roman civilization. In some places, functioning Roman legal and fiscal systems were also maintained, at least in the short to medium terms. Christianity and elite Latin culture survived as permanent defining features of all the continental successor kingdoms.

This negotiation was never cost-free for the Roman landowners (a reason to doubt that it should really be considered voluntary). The kings of the successor states had all been put in power by military followings, the more important of whom – numbering certainly in the thousands altogether across the different kingdoms – expected to be richly rewarded for the wars they had just waged to bring the new kingdoms into existence. And these military henchmen would not have had the slightest hesitation in replacing their leaders if the scale of the reward failed to match their expectations. Land was the only serious form of available wealth, which meant the successor-state kings required substantial portfolios of landed estates to satisfy their followers. There were some stocks of public land, but not enough to meet the scale of demand, so that in every kingdom Roman landowners had to surrender control of some of their holdings (the smaller the kingdom, the larger the percentage, as a basic rule of thumb). By sacrificing some of their estates in this way, Roman landowners south of the Channel managed to retain at least a portion of their wealth, and simultaneously transmitted a significant portion of their existing culture to the incoming barbarian elites, with whom they were now living cheek by jowl. Even the Vandal conquerors of North Africa, whose name has been synonymous with mindless violence since the eighteenth century, quickly learned to appreciate Roman villas and Latin poetry. A well-trained Latin poet who moved from northern Italy to Francia in the second half of the sixth century likewise found his verse equally popular at the courts of Clovis' grandsons among patrons of both Frankish and Roman descent. The ability of continental Roman landowners to negotiate their own survival at least ensured that the post-Roman West would be Latin and Christian.

Which is where the history of Britain diverges so fundamentally from the rest of the Roman west. The 'barbarian' Anglo-Saxon immigrants moving into fifth-century Britain were doing so in entirely different circumstances from their continental peers. The latter were on Roman soil involuntarily, responding to the exogenous shock delivered by the Huns. They also found themselves having to compete with a West Roman state which was still a substantial military power when they arrived in its territories in the first decades of the fifth century.

At that point, however, Britain had already partly separated itself from central Roman control, having declared independence in the middle of the extended period of disruption caused by the arrival of Radagaisus, the Vandal-Alans, and the Visigoths of Alaric (p. 90). This initial rebellion eventually led to the provincial Roman landowners of Britain, many of whom were still in place in the first few decades of the fifth century, being jettisoned from the imperial system completely, despite several subsequent appeals for central control to be restored, as their vulnerability became clear. They now had to organize their own defence against raiders from Scotland and Ireland who were queuing up for easy pickings, and were soon recruiting Anglo-Saxon warbands from across the North Sea to supplement their other available soldiery. The only credible narrative source reports that the situation really went downhill (probably in the early

440s) when these mercenaries realized there was nothing stopping them from taking full possession of their employers' land themselves, and recruited more continental warbands to join in the fun. As a result, small groups of Anglo-Saxon immigrants, under independent leaders, began to carve out their own little blocs of territory piecemeal. In this sense the Anglo-Saxons represent an extension of the kind of process which had previously seen empowered groups from the periphery take over imperial real estate between the Rhine and Danube and in Transylvanian Dacia in the third century.

It also meant that southern Britain never saw the kind of opportunity for large-scale negotiation that occurred on the continent, and no reason, either, for independent Anglo-Saxon warband leaders to unite under the authority of an overking, since there were no Roman imperial armies to fight. This generated a rolling process in which the entire Roman landowning class of Britain, together with its cultural values, were swept away, one villa at a time. By the time the last appeal for aid came into the West Roman centre, it was already under far too much pressure, having just lost North Africa to the Vandals, to find resources for the now beleaguered Romano-British landowners. What actually brought about Britain's post-Roman civilization collapse into an entirely pagan and Latin-free Dark Ages was not barbarian migration, but its voluntary severance from the Roman world: the original Brexit.

MIGRATION AND THE END OF EMPIRE

Only in the case of the Anglo-Saxons, therefore, do the realities of Roman-era migration come even close to traditional accounts of savage barbarians overwhelming a great civilization – and even the outcome in southern Britain had root causes which were not all about 'barbarian' violence. Elsewhere in the Roman West, where migration was largely the indirect product of the chaos generated by the Huns rather than predatory intrusion, the unfolding process was far from violence-free, but it produced negotiated outcomes which transferred significant features of the old imperial culture into the new world order. Even if this does not align with the received images of barbarian invasion which have attracted so much modern attention, these migratory patterns from the era of Roman collapse can be mobilized in a different way to help us understand the migration processes currently unfolding in and around the modern West.

To begin with it is important to recognize two inescapable features of human migration. First, it is hard-wired into the strategic life calculations of the species. Since the earliest diasporas ranged across Africa and into other continents, humans have consistently moved on in search of richer hunting grounds or better farmlands. Though they didn't always find them, expanded brain capacity has allowed humanity to use clothing, tools and food-processing technologies to bypass physical evolutionary adaptation, and flourish in a huge number of different environments across the planet. One clear conclusion to emerge from the comparative study of migration, therefore, is that there will always be a flow of population from poorer to richer areas so long as transport and information is available, and no political structures impose additional barriers. But, second, migration is never painless. For most migrants, leaving loved ones and home for strange new worlds is an emotional wrench, not to mention all the dangers and insecurities involved in the process. From killed or enslaved barbarians in the late-Roman period to dead children washing up on European beaches today, migration has never been without risks and sorrows.

Against this general backdrop of opportunity, necessity and difficulty, the life cycle of empires tends to generate some more specific patterns of movement. In their expansionary phases, as we have seen, empires deliberately provide conditions that facilitate large-scale migration of various kinds – new economic opportunities, security, transportation routes, even policies to encourage migration – with a view to securing benefits for the imperial core. Migrants may better themselves, but also the imperial structure as a whole. As the Roman Empire came into existence, Italy exported many individuals who helped develop the new provinces of the Empire. But these provinces also sucked in labour from beyond the frontier, by both voluntary and involuntary mechanisms. In the case of the modern West, the export of colonists from core areas in the era of expansion was similar in principle, but much more dramatic in practice. This was because the age of Western imperial expansion coincided with an extraordinary

demographic transformation, when medical and nutritional improvements combined with high birth rates to make Europeans – for one
unique historical moment – total an astonishing 25 per cent of the
world's population (Chapter 2). In that demographic context, there
was less need to draw labour into the empire's new provinces from
beyond the borders of the system, although that was still happening
to fill less desirable positions, as the phenomenon of slavery makes so
horribly clear.

Since 1945, however, the pattern has gone into reverse. Post-
imperial powers, like Britain, France and the Netherlands, opened
their doors to migrants from their former colonies. Other countries
which didn't have or had lost empires, like Germany, imported 'guest
workers' who were meant to return to their home countries (often
Turkey in the German case) at the completion of their working lives.
Understandably these 'guests' often stayed, since by then they had had
families who felt they belonged, not to mention national football
teams that didn't want to lose their best players. Meanwhile countries
which had always relied on immigration to swell their labour supply,
like the United States, Canada and Australia, found the traditional
European sources drying up, and turned increasingly to immigrants
from the developing world.

At first sight, with the barbarian invasions of the late Roman
period in mind, this could make it tempting to employ a wave metaphor to describe the relationship between Empire and migration,
supposing that it floods outwards during the ascendant phase of
empire before washing in as an Empire starts to decline. Such imagery
is prevalent in far-right discourses in some Western countries; they
compare the expansion of European culture across the globe during
the days of Empire, considering that an unproblematic 'good' thing,
to supposed current trends towards 'white genocide' in old colonial
possessions like South Africa and Rhodesia. They even warn – in the
most dramatic statements – of a possible 'white replacement' in the
West, as latter-day barbarians first reverse the advance of the West in
its colonies, and increasingly take the battle into the old heartlands of
Empire. The parallels between marauding Vandals and the rubble left
by Islamic State across much of the cradle of west Eurasian civilization in Syria and Iraq are seemingly inescapable. Today's immigrants

are the modern-day barbarians at the gate. Let them in and the in-evitable consequences will be loss of wealth, loss of cultural cohesion, and an upsurge of violence: at worst, even population replacement. But, despite winning some traction in disgruntled corners of different Western electorates, this kind of metaphor relies on a false equation. Even leaving aside its highly questionable value judgements, modern population flows into the West are the product of a fundamentally different relationship between migration and Empire to that which operated at the fall of the Roman Empire.

By the middle decades of the twentieth century, the European demographic explosion was coming to a close. The West's prosperity made it increasingly possible after 1945 for state structures to fund cradle-to-grave welfare systems, with generous pensions and health insurance. Individuals were much wealthier too. In the quarter-century after World War II, per capita incomes in Western countries grew on average between 4 and 6 per cent annually, which meant that individuals were seeing their incomes double every decade or so. As economic insecurity declined, family sizes correspondingly dimin-ished. There was no need to have lots of children to look after you in old age if the state, especially when supplemented by a private pen-sion, could do the job just as effectively. You could also now reckon that the vast majority of your children would actually survive. Fol-lowing the post-war baby boom, which brought about a short-lived jump, prevailing birth rates in the West therefore resumed their long-term decline; the second stage of the so-called 'fertility transition' was now in full flow. Since the war, the average number of children per household in the United States has halved. Today, of the developed countries of the OECD, only Icelandic and Israeli families produce enough children to maintain existing population levels (the replace-ment ratio generally being about 2.1 children per woman). Everywhere else, the native-born population is contracting, and precipitously so in the cases of Italy, Germany, Hungary and Japan.

As fertility rates in western Europe dropped sharply, most Euro-pean countries went far beyond losing their old role as significant providers of surplus population to the world economy, and began actually struggling to meet their own labour needs. The obvious source for extra supply was the developing world of the old imperial

periphery, because, in the decades from 1945, it too had finally begun
to experience the kind of spectacular population growth – caused by
the same medical and nutritional advances – that Europe had seen in
the later nineteenth century. By the mid-twentieth century, large pools
of surplus labour were to be found only in the developing world, and
the West responded accordingly. As a result, supposed analogies
between modern migration flows into the West and the so-called barbarian invasions of the late Roman period completely break down.

The migrations of the late fourth and early fifth centuries were
caused by an exogenous shock in the form of Hunnic expansion. The
process which unfolded subsequently on Roman soil was substantially
shaped by the migrants themselves, as they reorganized into ever larger
political confederations. This overall migratory process – both its origins and subsequent development – lay outside Roman control. The
vast majority of modern migration into the West, by contrast, has
been, and still is, controlled by recipient states in search of labour.
Even in immigrant-dense America, 'illegals' who have entered illicitly
make up less than 5 per cent of the total population.

So much of the discourse of right-wing politicians – like Nigel Farage cruising the English Channel to look out for migrant boats and
Boris Johnson citing the fall of the Roman Empire as a warning about
uncontrolled immigration in the present day or Pat Buchanan liken-
ing illegal immigrants to the Goths – is based on a false equivalence.
Nothing in the precarious existence of an undocumented labourer in
today's United States bears the slightest resemblance to a Vandal warrior enjoying the Roman good life in North Africa. An American
'illegal' lives in fear, always alert to where immigration enforcement
agents have been spotted, so that they can be avoided. Stigmatized,
their children often suffer a chronic fear of separation from deported
parents. And although the illegal immigrant and her family will probably experience much worse mental and physical health than a native
counterpart, their access to healthcare is constrained. Even when it is
available, immigrants often forgo using it for fear of being outed. For
all the talk of barbarians at the gates, the modern world offers not the
remotest parallel to the mass, organized, military confederations
which forced their way across the frontier and seized substantial
chunks of Roman real estate. After Hungary recently passed a law

that allowed its police to force asylum-seekers back over the border without due process, the number of people entering the country fell by over 75 per cent. The late Roman Empire could only have dreamed of halting the barbarian invasions by legislation.

Still more fundamentally, the relationship between migration and wealth in the ancient and modern cases is totally different. The organized mass migrations of the late Roman era had to generate major losses for somebody. Migrant Goths, Vandals, Anglo-Saxons and others were all competing for a share of the one main asset – land – and a share could be obtained only by taking it either completely (as in Britain) or partly (the continent) from its current holders, with the additional effect of – eventually – removing so much of the fiscal base from central control that the imperial state itself collapsed. Modern economies, by contrast, can grow in a way that was impossible in previous eras, so that wealth for new citizens doesn't have to be at the expense of existing ones. That's why, of course, post-1945 Western governments actually encouraged immigration. Given existing labour shortages, they judged that immigration had the capacity to *expand* the overall size of their economic and fiscal bases at their disposal.

By and large, that judgement has proved correct, even if recent research on the economic impact of immigration offers a more nuanced picture, with greater sensitivity to its uneven impact, than past celebrations of its unmitigated benefits. All things being equal, the wealthier elements in Western society have tended to benefit more from the arrival of immigrants than its traditional working class. A supply of immigrant labour does constrain wages that would otherwise rise in a more restricted labour market. There is now greater awareness, likewise, of the kind of policies needed to help migrants fully participate in a host economy: everything from skills training to language instruction. But even taking all this into account, research still generally indicates that, despite the claims of some Western politicians, immigration delivers a net gain to the entire economy. One mainstream IMF study estimates, for instance, that on average, every 1 per cent increase in the size of the immigrant population provides a 2 per cent boost to long-term GDP. And while anti-immigrant politicians will sometimes defend their position by saying they don't oppose immigrants per se, just 'bad immigrants' – by which they mean illegal or so-called 'unskilled' immigrants, though in practice this often amounts to the same thing – even unskilled immigrants provide more economic benefit than cost. In the United States, for instance, illegal immigrants comprise a higher share of the workforce than they do of the overall population, suggesting that a disproportionately high number of them are actively engaged in the productive economy.

Since 1945, therefore, immigrants have come to play a vital role in sustaining what remains of Western economic dynamism. But even this still fails to get to the heart of the total contribution of immigrants to life in the evolving West. In another, more immediate way, they now sustain the very lives of Westerners. To understand why, we need to return to the longer-term consequences of increased Western wealth and the fertility transition on average family size.

The unprecedented prosperity flooding through the West after 1945 quickly generated a paradox. It hastened the transition to smaller families, accelerating a decline in birth rates, while at the same time dramatically increasing average life expectancy. After the war, the average American lived to be sixty-seven; today, they make it to seventy-nine. But that improvement pales next to Italy's, where life expectancy rose from sixty to eighty-three over the same period, while in Japan the average person added a staggering thirty-two years to their then life expectancy of fifty-two. All of this is a wonderful achievement in so many ways. Longer, healthier, wealthier lives with more leisure time have much to recommend them. But they also have the economic drawback of reducing the percentage of the population actively engaged in the workforce at any one time.

Back in 1960, pensioners made up one-tenth of Japan's population. Today, they comprise nearly a third. The rise in the United States and Britain has been not quite so dramatic – from about 10 per cent again to about 15 per cent and 18 per cent respectively – but it's still substantial. As a result, the ratio of economic dependants to active workers has grown dramatically. Back in 1960, every economically active Japanese person supported one other person, and most of those were children soon to enter the workforce. Today, every worker must support two other people, and most of those are retired. Wealth and its effects have thus created massive new holes in the West's labour force, which immigration has again generally been used to fill.

In some areas of the economy, this dependency has become particularly heavy. With longer life has come a much greater incidence of the chronic health conditions associated with ageing: diabetes, arthritis, Parkinson's, dementia, you name it. In Britain, Nigel Farage made a career out of blaming the rising cost of Britain's National Health Service on excess demand generated by immigrants. He's right that the wards of Britain's hospitals are filled with foreigners – but most of them are healthcare professionals! Over one-third of the doctors working in the NHS come from abroad, which is broadly in line with the OECD average. This, of course, has a problematic flipside for the developing world, in that a fifth of the doctors graduating from African medical schools end up working overseas.

It isn't an influx of foreigners that's putting rising pressure on the West's welfare states, therefore, but the consequences of its own postwar prosperity, which has lengthened lifespans and massively increased dependency ratios. Relying on foreign-trained doctors and nurses has not just kept many public systems from collapsing – those in Australia and Canada would cease to function without them – but also off-loaded much of the cost of producing medical staff to other countries, saving Western taxpayers large sums of money, since every doctor costs upwards of $300,000 to train. Add in the migrants, both short-term and long-term, who play vital roles across the economy, from harvesting fruit up to running corporations, and it's hard to overestimate the economic role migration now plays in keeping the West in the style to which it has grown accustomed. As a result, both now and for the foreseeable future, the issue of migration presents Western governments with a completely different cost-benefit equation to that faced by their late Roman predecessors.

BUILD A WALL!

Substantial portions of different Western electorates have become hostile towards immigration. Worried about jobs, incomes and cultural cohesion, their fears are stoked by the sight of unruly migrant camps at the borders and occasional bursts of Islamist terror in Western cities. This antipathy has proved strong enough to effect some striking electoral successes – Brexit, Trump, the German far-right AfD, Viktor Orbán and others – prompting even some more mainstream politicians to seek ways to reduce their countries' dependence on foreign workers. In an era of ageing populations and increasing dependency ratios, however, any substantial reduction in immigration will necessarily have consequences for economic prosperity. After Brexit imposed limits on migration from Europe, Britain began to face chronic labour shortages which raised costs and dampened supply, as many people trying to do home renovations or waiting for luggage at an airport all too quickly discovered.

At one end of the spectrum of possible policy choices, Western countries could simply close the door to future immigration to preserve the socio-political and cultural status quo. Modern Japan has essentially taken this route, restricting immigration within tight limits by making it very difficult for migrant labourers to gain long-term residency status or bring their families to Japan. But the price has been high. Japan's economic growth more or less ground to a halt in the early 1990s, and has barely budged since, as its population ages and the demands placed on public services grow heavier. Highly restrictive immigration policies are a key reason why the number of Japanese retirees supported by the working population has increased far beyond the levels seen elsewhere in the developed world, to the point that today – with 30 per cent of its population in retirement – more than half of every yen brought in by taxation is consumed by the social-security budget. This requires the government to borrow heavily to pay for everything else, from teachers' salaries to rubbish collection. Halting migration absolutely thus seems to be a recipe for absolute economic decline (as well as experiments where old-age care is provided by robots). Japan's famed social cohesion and low crime rates show that this model has other potential benefits, but it comes with a hefty price tag, and even Japan has recently begun importing labour for its care homes and creating legal windows by which immigrants can gain permanent status.

A second, more commonly preferred policy option, therefore, has been to advocate keeping migration to within wider but still tight limits and, if possible, to favour source countries with an ethnic and cultural profile similar to that of the recipient country: hence Donald

Trump's notorious stated preference for migrants from Norway over 'shithole countries' in Africa. But counting on large-scale migration from other developed countries is unrealistic, because virtually every OECD country has been affected by the same fertility transition, and anyway there are no longer sufficient differences between their economic prospects to prompt migrants in large numbers to take on the cultural and personal costs of relocation. In reality, migration on any substantial scale can only come from parts of the periphery where the first stage of the fertility transition is underway – meaning that children are surviving in much larger numbers, but family sizes are only just beginning to adjust downwards in response.

Another proposed solution centres on so-called 'needs-based' migration regimes, where developed nations allow in carefully vetted migrants to fill specific skills shortages: a policy move which will not (supposedly) drive down wages or strain social systems. Some nationalist politicians use this idea as a proxy for generally reducing migration, but any pragmatically applied version of this policy would not drive down total migration at all. If Britain were to use a system like that of Canada or Australia, based on economic pragmatism, it would actually increase its intake of immigrants. Canada, which uses a fairly selective immigration policy to keep its labour force and dependency ratios in balance, generally imports about 1 per cent of its total population each year. Applied in Britain, which has twice the population of Canada, this would require 650,000 immigrants a year. Moreover, as the focus on 'essential' workers whose overall importance became so clear during the Covid crisis has emphasized, many vital members of the workforce are not highly skilled and yet still come from abroad, so that a selective immigration policy based on rational assessment rather than massaging electoral anxiety would also have to make proper allowance for shortages in unskilled labour. This point has recently been highlighted by the fact that the British government, after years of demonizing East European migrants, was reduced to begging them to return when they all went home at the height of the coronavirus pandemic, leaving British crops unharvested. Trying to resolve labour shortages and unfavourable dependency ratios 'rationally' might not, therefore, generate the kind of outcome that many Brexit voters had in mind when they voted to 'take back control'. Leaving the EU might slow down central and eastern European migration, but it is likely to replace it in due course with equivalent or larger flows from less developed parts of Africa, Asia, or South America.

If the large-scale 'barbarian' invasions of the late-Roman period in the end provide no kind of analogy for current immigration into the modern West, they can nonetheless be mobilized as an effective counterpoint through which to understand why not. The late Roman Empire saw a particular form of migration which quickly turned into an armed struggle for control of a fixed stock of landed assets. Immigration into the West since 1945, in stark contrast, has involved many more economic gains than losses for recipient countries, and the overall benefit has only increased as native Western populations age and dependency ratios increase. As with Japan, countries might nonetheless opt for very extensive immigration controls for cultural and political reasons, but tight immigration controls are bound to lower general standards of living over the longer term, in a context of ageing populations and flatlining productivity. Migration is not cost free, either for the immigrants, their host societies or the countries they leave, but at the very least politicians need to be much more honest about the trade-offs involved, and it would probably lead to better outcomes if they also at least occasionally referred to the most important modern migration story of all.

Over the last hundred years, the greatest ever known movement of people has indeed been underway, but only a small fraction of it has entered the West. The citizens of the developing world have been leaving their rural homes in truly astonishing numbers, far surpassing in scale even the largest 'barbarian' invasion of antiquity, but the overwhelming majority have ended up in nearby coastal and riverine cities. Places like Shenzhen, Sao Paolo, Lagos, Mumbai and hundreds of others have gone from colonial outposts to staggering metropolises in the space of just a few decades. It is this movement of people, many thousands of miles from Western borders, rather than the arrival in an ageing West of some much-needed recruits to its declining labour force, which poses the real migration-based challenge to continued Western prosperity and global influence.

7

Power and the Periphery

The year 1999, which featured Bill Clinton's triumphal State of the Union address, was shaping up to be a great one for him. Fresh from an impeachment acquittal, riding high in the polls as he sat astride a booming economy and soaring stock market, he aimed to close the year with an equally fitting finale: hosting the latest in a long line of global trade summits in Seattle, where he could celebrate the spread of the Western model across the global world.

For the half-century after 1945, Western governments had driven the global trade agenda, in keeping with the design of the Bretton Woods conference. The typical approach at GATT or its WTO successor had been for a handful of rich countries to hammer out a deal, then present it as a fait accompli to everyone else. By 1999, developing countries had long been hankering for a proper seat at the table, and the opportunity to put forward agenda items the United States persisted in excluding – above all the blanket refusal of developed countries to open up their agricultural markets. Unfortunately for Clinton, it was at this summit that things finally went off-script. As it opened, street protests, drawing together everyone from labour unions to environmentalists, shut down Seattle. Meanwhile a coalition of developing countries, led by some of the heavy hitters like India and Mexico, took a united stand against Clinton's attempts to steamroller through an agreement that once again largely ignored their demands. Many of them were still struggling under the austerity measures America had imposed as a condition for its help during the 1997–8 financial crisis. As the protests raged, the police declared a state of emergency and the National Guard rolled into town, while discussion ground to a halt in the conference halls. Clinton declared he could take things no further.

Instead of launching an invasion, the modern periphery had used diplomacy to fire a warning shot across the bows of the American-led Western Empire. For the first time in fifty years of trade talks, the imperial centre had been stopped in its tracks. What had changed?

GLOBALIZATION

Although the principal effect of the post-war global boom was to raise living standards in the West, it also increased demand for the raw materials produced in the less-developed economies of the old European colonies. The resulting economic growth didn't stop most Third World countries falling still further behind the West in rel-ative terms, because most of the newly independent states adopted inward-looking, protectionist development strategies, geared towards producing locally manufactured substitutes for the Western indus-trial goods they had imported in the colonial era. Designed to reinforce political with economic independence, such strategies had the paradoxical effect of hard-wiring under-development into the post-colonial periphery. The new local industries still relied on imported Western technology and machinery, so that strategy acci-dentally perpetuated the same old economic patterns: exporting primary goods – everything from foodstuffs to the raw materials used in Western factories – and using the revenues to buy industrial goods from the West.

By the 1970s, the post-war order was running aground. The often rapid expansion that followed independence, as the newly emergent countries rode the booming demand for their primary commodities and built their manufacturing sectors, had stopped generating high levels of growth once the import-substitution model reached its nat-ural limits. After national markets had been saturated, the only option for the new industries was to follow the primary-goods sectors and try exporting. But many of the factories had been equipped with second-hand, increasingly outdated machinery from the West, and they consequently struggled to compete in the markets of the world

economy without access to new technology, and the capital investment to acquire it.

In the West, the post-war boom was also subsiding. By the late
1960s, inflation, largely dormant since 1945, edged upwards, before
accelerating into terrifying double-digits, helped in part by the two oil
shocks of the 1970s. OPEC (the Organization of Petroleum Exporting Countries) had brought together a coalition of what were then
peripheral countries to control the flow of oil to the world economy,
driving a fourfold increase in the cost of a barrel of oil which sucked
out much more money from Western countries. Back in the West, this
also happened to be the moment when the growth in labour productivity started to decline, along with the proportionate size of the active
labour force (p. 107). Both developments put upward pressure on
labour costs. The end result was stagflation, a nightmare scenario of
little growth and high inflation which ruined the sleep of many a
1970s politician, from Prime Minister James Callaghan to President
Jimmy Carter. By the early 1980s, as Western economies sank into
recession, prices were rising by the month and mortgage rates were
climbing towards 20 per cent: Westerners were having to spend more
just as they were earning less, making it increasingly problematic for
governments to fund their cradle-to-grave welfare programmes.

After a host of failed initiatives, state subsidies and ineffective
nationalizations, a critical mass of Western politicians groped their
way towards a more radical solution, offered by an emerging consensus among so-called neoliberal economists such as Milton Friedman
and Friedrich Hayek. They proposed abandoning the dominant,
Keynesian model of economic management, slashing public spending
and substituting it with a hyper free-market approach instead, which
would encourage businesses to make the world their oyster. Since the
war, changes in technology had come together literally to lighten production and reduce the impact of distance on prices. In earlier
industrial eras, factories generally had to locate their operations close
to the source of their main raw materials and their principal markets
to limit expensive transport costs. But with the miniaturization of
components and the rise of plastics – bidding farewell to mid-century
televisions, for instance, which were wooden-encased behemoths
filled with clunky metal and glass parts – you could fit much more

value into a single shipment. The cost of shipping fell as well. The invention of the container – large steel boxes that were filled and sealed at their origin, remaining so until they arrived at their destination – meant not only that there was less 'slippage' (since the goods weren't handled, nothing could 'fall off the back of the lorry'), but also much less manpower involved in the process. Instead of the army of stevedores required to load and unload at every junction in a trade network, from lorry to train to ship and then back again, entire containers could be moved from one mode to another by a single crane operator. Finally, advances in communications technology, starting with the fax machine and progressing to the internet, made it possible to monitor an overseas supplier's operations in real time, allowing firms to move more and more of their operations to ever more distant locations.

Before businesses could take full advantage of this new age of technologically driven possibility, they had first to do away with the barriers and regulations that limited their overseas operations. Which is where the politicians became involved. From the late 1970s, starting with the elections of Margaret Thatcher and Ronald Reagan, Western governments began removing capital controls – which regulated the flow of cash across borders – and cutting taxes, while simultaneously using their diplomatic and financial leverage to press developing countries into opening their home markets to outside trade and investment. World Bank and IMF programmes to assist developing countries now began to attach so-called 'conditionality' clauses. In return for financial support, recipient governments were pressed into reducing barriers to trade, privatizing state companies or lifting regulations on markets, opening up their economies to foreign firms and investors.

The West was pushing at an open door. In the global periphery, governments were looking for new ways to meet the demands of growing populations for jobs, homes and services now that import substitution had hit the buffers. By this time, too, a domestic business class, which had initially looked to their governments to protect them from foreign competition at independence, was growing in confidence. Families like India's Tatas, who in the 1950s and 1960s had been content to shelter under the skirts of state protection while they built their operations, were ready to compete on a world stage. They particularly wanted to get their hands on foreign exchange, cheaper supplies and new markets, all of which required reduced public-sector control. The business elite found allies for this new orientation in the corridors of power, among politicians trying to attract new supporters and civil servants who were keen to shake things up. From Mexico to Mozambique, a generation of independence had produced a professional, technocratic elite of civil servants, many educated at Western universities, who were willing to experiment with new methods of economic management that advocated much less direct state control over the allocation of resources.

They also had an impressive example to imitate. After the war – faced with both the Soviet threat and, after the Communist take-over of mainland China in 1949, a seemingly ascendant communist bloc – the West, led by America, had sought to create a regional counterweight. They used trade policy to facilitate the economic growth of Japan and the Four 'Asian Tigers' of South Korea, Taiwan, Singapore and Hong Kong (then on lease from China to Britain). For political reasons, these states were all allowed to engage in 'unfair' trading practices, sheltering their own industries from import competition while still enjoying relatively unfettered access to Western markets. Rejecting the import-substitution model, these countries employed what came to be called the 'developmental-state' approach to growth. Nurturing a few key export industries, like cars and electronics, they opened up the rest of their economies to imports. The results were spectacular. At one point, the South Korean economy was doubling in size every six years (it's easy to forget that until the 1970s the Communist North was the richer of the two Koreas). This kept Western countries happy since they had swelling markets to sell to, not to mention friendly populations enjoying new-found prosperity.

Everything was set for a meeting of minds. Western governments were ready to let capital loose on the world, and their counterparts in the developing world were ready to make it easier for foreign, often Western firms to use their workers to assemble imported parts into finished goods for re-export. This was achieved either by setting up overseas subsidiaries, or by contracting with local businesses like the Tatas. The final element underpinning the economic explosion which followed was the phenomenon with which we closed the previous chapter: the largest human migration the world has ever seen.

In the decades after 1945, many major cities of the periphery had filled with a tide of rural migrants, who came looking for the opportunities that independence had seemed to promise. Completely dwarfing the corresponding migration flow into the West, this meant that many (particularly coastal) cities of the developing world were already swollen with hundreds of millions of migrants from the countryside as the tide of globalization started to roll in. They'd come looking for work in their countries' nascent industrial sectors, but import-substitution generated only limited employment, so few had enjoyed much success. What they did usually get, however, was a basic education, since post-colonial governments invested heavily in schools and universities. As the West deregulated, developing countries could offer its firms access to vast pools of labour equipped with basic skills and literacy, at a fraction of the cost of their Western counterparts: the same job sometimes being done for one fiftieth of the price.

The neoliberal globalization of the Reagan-Thatcher era opened up this teeming labour market to Western firms. Companies began shifting labour-intensive assembly processes, like textile weaving or the production of car parts, to the Third World, while retaining more highly skilled office jobs like design, engineering and management back home. Over time, the neoliberal world view moved beyond its original partisans in the West's conservative parties and found considerable acceptance on the left as well. Whether in the form of Bill Clinton's or Tony Blair's 'Third Way', the 'new middle' of Germany's economic Hartz reforms early this century – which sought to 'encourage' job-seekers into work by reducing their benefits – or more recently Emmanuel Macron's reform programme in France, cutting taxes and changing labour laws, Keynesianism was supplanted as the dominant economic doctrine of the West. In place of a benevolent state that aimed to manage the economy so that businesses and citizens could prosper, everything was now to be left to a free market in which 'enlightened self-interest' resulted in socially beneficial outcomes. A key element of the neoliberal model was a renewed stress on education, the idea being that those left unemployed in the West by the collapse of old industries could acquire new, more marketable skills: enter the cliché of coal-miners learning to code. And since most of the developing world had opened itself up by the early 1990s, the whole industrial process which had made the West so dominant was reorganized on a global scale and at breakneck speed. Private Western investors, including huge institutional players like the vast pension funds that had grown up in the post-war period, needed higher returns to support promises made to their clients, and eagerly provided the necessary capital to advance the process.

In the short term these revolutionary manoeuvres had the desired effect of restoring corporate profits in the West, and hence of boosting share values and tax revenues. This allowed Western governments to maintain and even expand social spending if they chose to. Liberal-izing trade and outsourcing production also enabled politicians who were struggling to raise wages at least to keep inflation down, since everyone could now buy cheaper Asian imports instead of expensive home-made products. In effect, the economic calculations underlying modern global trading patterns had evolved into the mirror image of their ancient Roman predecessors. In the Roman world, transport costs were everything and labour cheap, so goods were made as close as possible to the point of consumption. In the era of globalization, transport costs became minimal – all those massive bulk carriers manned by several computers and a couple of dozen people – and labour costs everything, so goods were made where labour was cheap and then shipped to the rest of the planet. In its early years, and par-ticularly during the 1990s, this new international order seemed to work for everyone. The Third World prospered, while Western stock markets soared.

Not all peripheral societies benefited. In some cases, politicians' greed carried the day. The wealth of Zaire (now the Democratic Republic of Congo) was plundered for over thirty years by its long-time leader, Mobutu sese Seko, while Venezuela under Nicolas Maduro would offer the world a textbook example of how not to run an economy, depressing growth and driving up inflation, with chronic shortages resulting. Even in those countries which were profiting under better leadership, the paternalism characteristic of the import-substitution era quickly gave way to more competitive, insecure social systems, in which people were left increasingly to fend for themselves. Nevertheless, wherever the developing world responded positively to the new possibilities, economic growth usually accelerated, creating new business and employment opportunities. Whereas it had long been assumed that the slower growth of the periphery was a chronic condition, and that these societies would remain forever poorer than those of their old imperial masters, a new picture started to emerge. The growth of the periphery, it became clear, was slower only because it started later. Through the 1980s and 1990s many developing countries began trading more and more with the outside world (the increase being dramatic in countries like South Korea and India), and in the fastest-growing societies the gains were sufficiently broad-based to create a new middle class of global consumers.

Below the surface, however, this rising tide of peripheral prosperity was decisively altering the course of Western global domination, in much the same way that long-term economic and demographic expansion in northern Europe eventually undermined the ancient balance of power which had underpinned the rise of Rome. In the century either side of the birth of Christ, a Mediterranean resource base had been sufficient to allow Rome to make huge conquests across northern Europe. As they became more fully developed, however, the resources of the north allowed the imperial periphery first to push back against the centre's domination, and then to dominate the Mediterranean itself from a new location. In a similar way, if operating at the much faster pace of industrial rather than agricultural development, the Bretton Woods system, which had so powerfully served Western interests after 1945, had been crafted at a moment of unprecedented American strength. After 1980, the new economic heft of the periphery began altering this power balance in subtle but significant ways. Several developing countries, including India, Brazil, Pakistan and Mexico, began to position themselves more effectively to exert greater influence and build alliances at international meetings. Not only were they more capable and committed to getting better deals for themselves and other developing countries, but to an increasing extent they now had important bargaining chips: the access to their markets that Western countries so keenly sought.

Given these trajectories of development, it was just a matter of time before developing governments converted greater economic power and governmental sophistication into upgraded political influence. In the streets of Seattle that autumn afternoon, crowds from Western civil-society groups came out en masse to protest at what they saw as the iniquities and inequities of neoliberal globalization in their own societies. But the real action was taking place indoors, in the conference venue. There, as tear gas choked the streets outside, a nascent coalition of developing countries, alienated by all the US-led backroom dealing, shut the 1999 WTO Summit down by refusing to deal. When it finally resumed two years later in Doha, the coalition made it address an entirely different agenda, with much greater attention to the concerns of developing countries. The global order created in 1945 to maintain Western dominance in an era of formal decolonization had suffered a fatal blow.

But, as was the case with ancient Rome, a noisily assertive inner periphery was not actually the West's biggest problem. In the deeper past, the rise of the north in the first millennium changed the European balance of power forever, making a Mediterranean-based Empire no longer viable, but it did so over the long term. Anglo-Saxon infiltration in southern Britain and Frankish expansion west of the Rhine were, as we have seen, a relatively small part of the story of Roman imperial collapse. Much more important was the pressure of the Huns from the outer periphery which prompted the rise of new coalitions on Roman soil. In the same way, while globalization undermined the post-war settlements enacted at Bretton Woods, this hardly amounted to a geostrategic revolution. At the same time as globalization was remaking the economies of the old inner periphery, however, a much greater threat to the West's continued global domination was emerging in territories that had only ever belonged to the outer periphery of the Western imperial system.

CHINA SYNDROME

With an average of roughly one in every four humans living within its borders for most of recorded history, China had always been the world's largest economy until the ascent of the West and its own decline after 1800. Repeatedly humiliated by Western powers, imperial China descended into internal warfare, while late nineteenth-century efforts to reform and modernize its structures, following the lead of contemporary Japan, were eroded by the corruption of powerful vested interests. As a result, China had the painfully unusual distinction of seeing its economy fall backwards in this era, not just relative to an ascendant West, but in absolute terms, as much of its population sank into poverty. By the time of the 1949 Communist Revolution, the Middle Kingdom had become a shadow of its former self. Mao Zedong's subsequent attempts to build a closed, self-sufficient economy only reinforced backwardness. On his death in 1976, the country's per capita income stood at about $200 per annum, less than a fortieth of that in America. In the intervening decades, China had been operating largely separately from the post-war Western Empire, with only marginal engagement in its economic structures, which saw less than one-tenth of its total GDP traded externally.

After Mao's death, things turned around dramatically – though the change was scarcely noticeable at first. After a frenetic few weeks, a new group of reformers led by Deng Xiaoping took power in Beijing, ousting the more hard-line Communist Gang of Four, who included Mao's widow Jiang Qing. Officially, China remained on the course Mao had set for it, with his portrait still looming large over Tiananmen Square. Unofficially, Deng started a revolution – albeit gingerly – beginning with some agricultural reforms in 1978, and then gradually gathering pace as the government progressively liberalized industry and trade. By the 1990s, the country was fully back on the world stage, and the share of its economic output which it bought or sold abroad had quadrupled in just fifteen years. The Chinese economy boomed, matching the stellar record of the Four Asian Tigers. By 2016, the average Chinese person was twenty-five times richer in real terms than forty years before, with a per capita income that was now over a quarter of that of America's (and rising). China's share of global industrial production, negligible in 1976, rose correspondingly to nearly one-quarter, and today the country is – or soon will be, depending on which measure you use – the world's largest economy.

The significance of this extraordinary sea-change in world history can hardly be overstated. The full consequences are still working themselves out, but such a revolutionary transformation in the distribution of global economic power will necessarily have enormous, and parallel, political consequences. For the first time, essentially, the Western Empire now finds itself facing a genuine peer superpower competitor. The old Soviet Union never had the economic clout to match its military ambitions and was unable to extend its global influence by providing economic support to more than a handful of overseas clients (p. 75). Nor, despite renascent Cold War rhetoric, have Vladimir Putin's attempts to restore Russia's greatness done much to change this. The Russian economy is run largely on oil and gas sales, which was already a risk over the longer term as the world transitions away from fossil fuels. The economic implosion which resulted from the imposition of Western sanctions after Putin's 2022 invasion of Ukraine highlighted just how fragile and limited the Russian economic base is. Meanwhile the country's successes at undermining Western democracies via cyber warfare, which have been at times impressive, nonetheless ultimately depend on the co-operation of more and less willing Western stooges, whether to dump emails, fund destabilizing political campaigns or recirculate fake news. Even Russia's much vaunted military machine, when unleashed on neighbouring Ukraine's much smaller military, revealed itself to be lumbering, outdated, and often inept.

China presents a completely different picture. If its military is still untested in major conflict, its share of global GDP currently stands in the region of 16 per cent (compared to 2 per cent for Russia). Its authoritarian government has also been able to limit both private consumption and public spending on areas such as welfare, which leaves it free to direct nearly half of the economy's total economic output towards new investments. This is an astounding figure which is roughly double and even triple – in the case of a laggard like Britain – most Western countries, among whom even the frugal Swiss barely reach a third. It also means that China has lots of spare cash available for projecting power overseas.

So far, China's renewed superpower status, intertwining with the economic momentum that was already building up in much of the developing world, has mostly expressed itself in the arenas of soft power. If still Western-dominated, the global financial system has come to depend increasingly on financial flows from the developing world, with Hong Kong, Singapore, Shanghai and Dubai becoming banking centres on a par with the old financial capitals of London, New York and Zurich. And in an era when the West has generally been cutting aid budgets, China has stepped in to fill the vacuum, boosting its foreign assistance to win numerous diplomatic allies. You only have to wander around Addis Ababa or Lusaka, with their extensive new high-rise offices, shopping complexes, and Chinese-built roads, to see how rapidly China is expanding its footprint on the African continent in particular. As a result, one government after another has abandoned Taiwan, the breakaway province to which the Nationalist government under Chiang Kai-shek retreated at the time of the Communist Revolution, recognizing Beijing and not Taipei as the one true Chinese government.

More recently, though, a harder edge to rising Chinese power has begun to reveal itself. The country has abandoned the old mass conscription people's army of the Maoist period to generate smaller, more specialized armed forces equipped with the latest technology. In the last few years it has built two aircraft carriers (with another four in the pipeline), a string of militarized artificial islands close to home, and a series of military bases across Asia and the Indian Ocean. As it steps up military exercises off Taiwan and tightens its hold on Hong Kong, China is using its military assets to assert regional influence, to the consternation of neighbouring Asian governments and the United States, whose own influence is declining in consequence. Just like its Roman predecessor in the third century, the modern Western Empire now faces its own superpower competitor. And even if, like Sasanian Persia, the rise of China has not immediately undermined the West's own superpower status, it does pose a series of direct and indirect challenges which sooner or later will have to be met.

BEYOND THE END OF HISTORY?

In 1992, having seen the Berlin Wall get ripped down, Francis Fukuyama famously declared that we had reached the 'end of history'. He claimed that the Western model of liberal democracy was now so dominant worldwide that mankind's ideological evolution had come to its natural conclusion. We were all going to end up as liberal democratic capitalist states. Even at the time, this sounded hubristic. Today it looks delusional. The startling economic rise of much of the old inner periphery on the back of the dramatic internal migration of the last few decades, and China's explosion onto the world stage from the outer periphery, makes it clear that, if Western global domination has not been overturned, it is certainly being challenged, and effectively so, for the first time. Nor is there the slightest chance that any of these developments will prove ephemeral. Just as the global rich-list has now started to be populated by billionaires from the global south, whose numbers increase each year, so too have many peripheral economies gone from perennial stragglers to among the most dynamic on the planet. As a result, *all* of the world's fastest-growing economies now belong to the former periphery. China's return to the centre of the global economy is a hugely important phenomenon, but the overall challenge to the West is so much more than a Chinese story. In recent years India's annual economic growth rate, long derided for sluggishness, has overtaken China's, while, in 2019, six of the world's fifteen fastest-growing economies were African. Africa still conjures up stereotyped images of famine and disease in Western minds, but a new reality of economic convergence is dawning.

The evident dynamism of the Chinese economy and the wider developing world, compared to declining growth rates in the West, has also occasioned some serious soul-searching about the failings of democracy and the supposed superiority of authoritarian systems. While autocrats may have their drawbacks, one line of thought has it, at least they get things done, and the ham-fisted response of some Western governments to the coronavirus pandemic has only strengthened such opinions. Most of the world's new wealth is being generated outside the old imperial core, and Western values are consequently losing their lustre even among some Westerners, despite the fact that the West still accounts for a majority of global GDP and that some of the most successful East Asian responses to the coronavirus challenge happened in democracies, like South Korea and Taiwan. Rather than continuing to subscribe to Fukuyama's unconvincing triumphalism, or following the current (equally uncritical) fashion for autocracy, Roman history offers us an alternative way to think through what might happen next.

Looking at the different stages in the Roman Empire's relations with the world around it, it is initially tempting to think that the modern Western Empire has now evolved to the point that its ancient counterpart had reached in the later third and fourth centuries. This was the era when Persia had once again become a superpower competitor, and the European peripheries of the Empire were on the rise. That would be challenging enough but, on closer inspection, current circumstances actually look much more like the still more precarious situation of the 420s, when the new confederations had already established permanent settlements on Western soil. That's not because 'barbarian' immigrants are moving into the modern West in increasing numbers. Today's immigrants generally support rather than threaten the economies and societies of the developed world (Chapter 6). The real parallel here lies in remembering *why* those fifth-century settlements, largely of displaced groups from the inner periphery, were such a problem for ancient Rome. Agricultural land was its fundamental means of generating wealth. The 'barbarian' settlements directly undermined the imperial system by removing a significant percentage of the total stock of wealth-generating assets from its control, leaving the central state to try to fulfil its duties to its citizens on a much-reduced income.

In the modern case, the ex-colonial periphery will have no reason to invade the core because the same overall effect is being achieved by the transfer to the periphery of control of a significant portion of the wealth-generating assets of the modern world: in this case the machinery of industrial production rather than agricultural land. Instead of organizing armies of soldiers, the states of the modern periphery have organized armies of workers. In both cases, the asset transfers began as policies adopted in response to serious crises. But short-term responses to immediate crisis often have longer-term and unforeseen consequences.

In the Roman case, the initial settlements in Spain and Gaul in the 410s were a way of dealing with migrants displaced by the rise of the Huns. The settlements created powerful peripheral entities on Roman soil, but, at that point, the imperial centre remained the strongest power by some distance within the Western Empire as a whole. When such settlements spread to North Africa in the 430s, however, the balance of economic and hence political power swung substantially further away from the centre. This process then continued until, after the failure of Constantinople's last attempt to rescue the West in 468 by destroying the Vandal kingdom in North Africa, the rising peripheries (Visigoths, Vandals and Burgundians in the lead) were quickly able to overturn the last vestiges of central influence by seizing control of what remained of its wealth-generating agricultural lands. Is the modern West destined to follow a similar trajectory to effective disappearance by losing control of a critical mass of its productive assets?

The relative decline of the modern West, and the potential threat posed by a resurgent China, has already prompted two broad responses from Western governments, who find it hard not to pine for the status quo ante or at least something more like it. The Trump presidency sought to undermine China's growing soft power by clipping its economic wings, a strategy explicit in its efforts to drive harder trade deals. In addition, several Western governments have sought to reassert their military presence to rein in what they perceive as Chinese adventurism; Britain's defence secretary announced in 2019 that he would send the country's new aircraft carrier into the South China Sea. As China expands its footprint in its immediate vicinity, bringing it dangerously close to a long-standing American sphere of influence in the Pacific, tensions are bound to rise. The most pessimistic voices have even warned of an impending 'Thucydides Trap': the supposed rule that a declining, previously pre-eminent power will at some point turn to war with a rising competitor.

As appealing as such hard-headed approaches may be to some Western audiences, they have yet to bear much fruit. The Chinese government quickly slapped down the buccaneering British defence secretary, reminding London in no uncertain terms that he was no longer living in the nineteenth century. Back then, Britain preached a gospel of free trade precisely because it had the gunboats to force Chinese markets to accept its industrial products and Indian opium. Today, Britain needs Beijing's permission to enter Chinese markets, and its eagerness to secure a post-Brexit trade deal with China quickly forced the British government to back down and toast the two countries' 'strong and constructive relationship' – while clarifying that the aircraft carrier wouldn't be going anywhere for at least a couple of years.

Even though the United States has a lot more weight to throw around than Britain, it's not clear what it would gain from doing so. Donald Trump promised it would be 'good and easy' to win a trade war with China, but it ended up hurting the US more. The then president claimed that the tariffs he imposed in 2018 to force China back to the bargaining table would be paid for by Chinese firms, but Americans got stuck with the bill, in the form of higher prices, reduced exports, and an estimated 300,000 jobs lost in the course of the standoff. And whereas American industrial production fell during the dispute, China just replaced lost US sales with exports into other markets. Given how closely intertwined America's economy has become with China's over the last few decades, any possible economic harm the US could inflict on its rival would be bound to produce matching collateral damage at home.

Here, the main lesson Roman history has to offer is that outright confrontation with a superpower competitor is not a good way to preserve what remains of your own pre-eminence, in an era when other developments are challenging the maintenance of your global power. Rome and Persia never liked each other. They quarrelled over borders, trade links, and the control of clients; they also trumpeted competing ideologies. Both claimed to be uniquely supported by different all-powerful divinities, which made for ultimately incompatible world views. But, once it had become clear by the end of the third century that neither had the power to subjugate the other, conflict was generally confined to a series of squabbles over short-term bragging rights, which didn't attack the vital workings of either system. And when both were simultaneously threatened by intrusive nomad powers from the steppe in the late fourth and fifth centuries, they shifted from mutual suspicion to positive cooperation: recasting each other as the 'twin lights of the firmament' (as one Roman emperor put it) and consistently refusing to quarrel over the same issues which had previously seen them at loggerheads.

When the nomad menace receded again around the year 500,

Rome and Persia soon returned to the old patterns of confrontation. The Roman Emperor Justinian (527–65) showed a particular propensity for aggression in a reign remarkable for military adventurism. This just about worked for him (despite some major losses, he scored enough victories to be able to claim that God supported his rule), but, in the longer term, his exploits gave an impetus to escalating confrontation, with both empires abandoning their old restraint, and instead seeking much bigger wins. This culminated in twenty-five years of total war at the start of the seventh century (603–27), which eventually ended in stalemate with both empires utterly bankrupt. The resulting power vacuum was immediately exploited by the newly united Islamic Arab world to change the face of Mediterranean and Near Eastern history irrevocably. The Persian Empire was completely extinguished by the early 650s, and Constantinople, as we've seen, lost so much territory that it was reduced from global Empire to regional power.

The message here is a simple one, but salutary. Chinese power is not going away, and confronting it head-on, economically or politically, will surely be counterproductive. Modern weaponry means that superpower conflict could destroy not only the main protagonists but the entire planet. And even much more limited forms of sustained confrontation would likely undermine any possibility of cooperation in the face of a range of pressing global issues which self-evidently require a collaborative approach: not least pollution, population, disease and global warming. Western governments will do best carefully to pick their battles, therefore, confronting Beijing only where Chinese behaviour threatens either cherished Western principles or a stable global order, as with the country's treatment of ethnic minorities, its possible violations of international law or treaties – Hong Kong looming large in this discussion – or its increasing hostility towards Taiwan (and even then it can expect tough negotiations, since the differences between the sides on some of these issues are existential to the Chinese).

The Chinese will also need to exploit one of their most strategic assets, which their behaviour, until very recently, has been tending to undermine: their alliances. Whereas most Western countries belong to large and powerful military alliances, China acts alone. Diplomatic coordination among countries with differing interests is never easy, but it will arguably bear more fruit than the go-it-alone methods favoured recently in Trump's America or Brexit Britain. Britain's withdrawal from the EU, for instance, meant that its 'strategy' (for want of a better word) to modernize its communications infrastructure using cheap Chinese technology fell hostage to its equally pressing need to curry favour with a US administration from which it wanted a trade deal. Going it alone as a small to medium power usually means weakening yourself in the face of the really big battalions. Much more effective is the kind of united Western response that followed Putin's invasion of his Ukrainian neighbour, when the Western allies coordinated rapidly to agree common positions which resulted in huge flows of military and other aid to Ukraine, and the imposition of devastating sanctions on the Russian economy.

Given all the economic and political power that has been building up in the old imperial periphery in the last few decades, the obvious additional move would be to try to expand existing Western alliance systems by recruiting the many developing countries which, at least notionally, share Western structures of democracy and freedom, such as India, South Africa and Brazil, and in doing so build a larger coalition of peer states. Some of these (particularly India) anyway have their own reasons for wanting to insure themselves against unfettered Chinese power. To do so would mean accepting some curtailing of traditional Western global domination, but this approach offers a better chance of preserving the best of Western values into the unavoidable post-imperial era.

The great gain of such an approach today would be to build a more effective counterweight to China in international negotiations. To succeed, though, this strategy would require more, not less, openness on the part of Western countries, and probably also substantial aid to bolster these diplomatic undertakings. One reason China has been securing so many favourable trade deals and investment opportunities across the developing world is that it is more willing to shower largesse than many Western countries. Building a meaningful engagement with the old periphery is a more promising way forward, but would cut against the grain of current Western political discourse, which wants to slash aid budgets to concentrate assistance at home or benefit home-country exporters. The British government's 2020 decision to close down its foreign-aid agency – widely admired as one of the world's most effective, now folded into an already overstretched foreign ministry – but carry on with building its aircraft carrier probably won a few votes in Tory shires. In global terms, however, it amounted to dispensing with one of Britain's most potent tools of soft power to brandish a hard power that looked decidedly limp: lacking the jets to use it, the carrier's flight deck was loaned to the Americans.

It's not just a question of cash. With authoritarian politics on the rise in many Third World democracies, Western politicians who want to re-orient their foreign relations in a more engaging manner are likely to face another challenge. All of the main potential targets for such overtures have good historical reasons – several centuries of exploitative domination – for suspecting Western motives. During the Ukraine war, for example, there was lots of talk in Western capitals of how Russia was totally isolated in the world. But in fact, more than half of humanity is represented by governments which abstained in the main UN General Assembly vote condemning Russia. In Africa, many people and governments saw little to be gained from taking sides in a conflict involving a country with which they have no quarrel, and which (as the old Soviet Union) supported their independence struggles against the very countries now demanding their solidarity.

The same historical backstory at least partially explains the success China has had in building warm relations with many developing countries. While China is often criticized for turning a blind eye to human rights abuses in the countries to which it provides assistance, its studied commitment to the principle of non-intervention goes down well in many developing countries with fresh memories of the Western colonial alternative. This is particularly true when the West can still produce leaders who make jaw-dropping – to say nothing of historically illiterate – statements like Africa 'may be a blot, but it is not a blot upon our conscience' as a future British prime minister did in 2002, suggesting that the continent's principal problem was that Britain no longer ruled it. Most Africans, by contrast, are well aware that they've had to start building their countries on the back of a long history of economic exploitation and political repression, which helps explain why the Western alliance found it hard to muster much African enthusiasm for its 2022 efforts to isolate Russia. Where was the equivalent support, they could justly complain, when we were trying to isolate apartheid South Africa?

If Western countries want to check Chinese expansion in the global periphery, the Western narrative will need to change, moving away from an implicit determination to preserve Western greatness at the expense (if need be) of developing countries, and towards assisting them to strengthen both their overall prosperity and their social and governmental structures. Effectively, this would mean widening the small club of the old imperial core to include a larger range of voices in international organizations and negotiations, on considerably more equal terms than those implicitly offered in Clinton's approach to the 1999 Seattle Summit (indeed, some of the summit's rebel leaders might make good candidates for membership).

The only plausible leader and coordinator for such an enlarged – more generally democratic and based on the rule of law rather than just being Western – bloc would still be the United States, which, to perform such a role consistently, would have to damp down its own long-standing isolationist tendencies in favour of the much larger potential gains of cooperation. The other governments of the old Western Empire would also have to commit the appropriate level of resources to the project for it to work, and to make it easier to sell to American electorates. As the recent experiences of NATO and the European Union reveal, to say nothing of WTO discussions since the Seattle Summit, preserving cohesion amid enlargement is a challenge that asks a huge amount of diplomacy, because the discussion has to include a larger number of often contending voices. But the alternative, where each state goes it alone, while making it easier for an individual country to reach decisions, will also mean that those decisions will amount to little of any value.

Greater participation in a broader international bloc, open to discussing the needs of its enlarged membership on more equal terms, would also provide a mechanism for some of the better products of modern Western civilization to become hard-wired into the new global order. Although the West used the wealth of others to fund their development, concepts like the rule of law, relatively impartial and efficient public institutions, a relatively free press, and properly accountable politicians massively enhance the overall quality of life in any country. Thus, some of the West's fiercest critics object not to the Western values of individual liberty and democracy, but to the fact that the West has not always practised what it preached in the rest of the world. A hard-headed focus on these kinds of solid values, while being more open, simultaneously, to accepting the legitimacy of non-Western concerns, will have a lot more traction among the citizens of the rising periphery than nostalgia for the former supposed glory of Western world domination, which goes down well with certain sections of Western electorates.

As we saw in Chapter 5, the continuation of Roman civilization was only made possible through negotiation. On the continent, negotiation between elites and emergent dynasts meant the new order of the post-Roman West incorporated some characteristic Roman features, such as Latin literacy, Christianity, and a tradition of written law. It is important not to idealize the significance of these cultural forms. They were important primarily to Roman elites, and survived because they subsequently proved equally attractive to the non-Roman elite that quickly emerged. The contrast with the outcome north of the Channel, however, could not be more striking, where no members of the Roman landowning elite found a pathway into the new order, and all the characteristic features of Roman life disappeared. In the end, some of these (Christianity, written law and Latin literacy) were reintroduced into Anglo-Saxon England from the end of the sixth century, when its kings, inexorably attracted by the developing economic networks of metropolitan Europe next door, found that cultural assimilation was the best path to cutting the best deals. That would not have happened, however, if these old Roman values had not managed to cement themselves already into the rest of the post-Roman West.

For Western states today to negotiate successfully, it will also be crucial for them to adopt a nuanced position towards China itself. They need to separate Chinese policies which threaten what's best in the Western tradition from those reflecting China's perfectly legitimate desire to resume its accustomed place as one of the world's great powers and overturn some of the remaining detritus of arrogant

Western imperialism. While periodic confrontation surely will be a feature of the relationship, reverting to a uniformly hostile Cold War-style rhetoric would be self-defeating. Economic, political and cultural cooperation will also need to be consistent features of any successful policy mix. For all its growing assertiveness, China's belligerence doesn't yet reach far outside its immediate neighbourhood. Before making grandiose statements, for instance, Western defence ministers might first ask themselves how they'd feel if China announced it would soon be sending an aircraft carrier into the English Channel or the Caribbean Sea. Ringed by unfriendly rivals, from the US Pacific Fleet to neighbours like India and Vietnam with whom it has fought wars in living memory, it is to be expected that China will feel the need to defend its growing economic prosperity with a stronger defensive perimeter.

So far, at least, there is a strong case to be made that China's growing military footprint simply mirrors its growing economic footprint, and the picture of Chinese aggression is sometimes complicated by the fact that it is confronting neighbours whose own behaviour sometimes suggests less than benign intent. Depending on one's vantage point, China's 2020 border fight with India could be seen as either an offensive measure or a pre-emptive strike against an increasingly contentious and chauvinistic government in Delhi. Fundamentally, the exceptional global role as policeman of world order that America was able to assume after World War II reflected a brief and exceptional power vacuum in Asia. With China returning to its historic place, America's own military footprint will inevitably have to wane now proportionately, but by no means disappear as a prop to continued peace and stability, especially if a network of alliances can be constructed to balance but not directly threaten China's position.

The sheer scale of China, and its growing economic and diplomatic influence across the developing world, suggest it will be impossible to avoid getting it on board with any strategy of transition into a new global political architecture, despite the undeniable institutional and ideological differences. As humbling as this might be to Western countries which not that long ago were telling China what to do, history suggests the alternative is far worse. The current global context offers much greater and more threatening challenges than the nomads who pushed Rome and Persia towards greater cooperation. Any enlarged American-led alliance would do very well to cast itself as fundamentally cooperative in its attitude to China, the twin light of the modern global firmament, despite the fact that there will undoubtedly be conflict and tension. The broader potential gains of such an approach go far beyond economics. It's hard to see how climate change and the further consequences of demographic revolution can possibly be effectively tackled without a broadly global approach. Preventing any further tragedies of the kind that beset Libya, Afghanistan and Syria when their fragile governments collapsed, likewise, would be much easier in a context more prone to cooperation than confrontation. Already Europe showed itself to have learned from the mistakes of its chaotic, each-state-for-itself approach to the 2015 refugee crisis with its coordinated, and highly effective, approach to the 2022 wave of Ukrainian refugees.

As they enter the third decade of the third millennium, therefore, Western countries find themselves facing multiple challenges as they contemplate the new world order emerging around them. Much as, centuries before, Rome faced both Persia and frontier confederations, China's rise means that the Western bloc of nations now has to deal with both a rival superpower for the first time, and irreversible processes of development in the former imperial periphery that have created important new voices with enough economic and political clout to demand a serious hearing. Much the easiest response to sell to home audiences still schooled in colonial history is confrontation, in economic and probably political terms as well. But this has major, potentially ruinous costs, compared to the more realistic but less immediately popular approach of accepting the inevitability of the periphery's rise and trying to engage with it.

The short answer to the question with which this book began, therefore, is straightforward. The West cannot make itself great again in the old terms. The tectonic plates of economic organization on which those political structures rested have shifted decisively, and nothing is going to move them back. Western politicians need to tell their citizens the truth about this, and get on with constructing the new, less self-aggrandizing world order which would in fact defend their (and everyone else's) interests more effectively.

If they fail to do so, prioritizing confrontation to prop up the global position of the Western world in the short term, the longer-term consequences are likely to be disastrous. For while the geo-strategic consequences of globalization are challenging enough, a second fundamental threat to Western values over the next few decades is likely to originate much closer to home.

8

Death of the Nation?

On 23 June 2016, 72.2 per cent of the British electorate turned out to vote by a narrow margin – 51.9 per cent to 48.1 per cent – to leave the European Union. Most immediately, this was a victory for the Brexit campaign, the combined brainchild of Conservative politicians and the Vote Leave organization, but the vote also revealed a deep divide among the British voting public. There is a 'middle' which is not particularly vested in either position, but this sits between pro- and anti-constituencies whose battlelines remain sharply drawn. Half a decade of subsequent manoeuvring only sharpened the divide. Nor is Britain alone in the striking lack of consensus marking its current political discourse. In the United States, Trump election rallies in 2016 greeted mentions of his opponent Hillary Clinton's name with cries of 'Lock her up', his electoral base responding enthusiastically to their champion's deliberately divisive political messaging. In winter 2018–19, likewise, France's major cities were rocked by months of violent street protests on the part of the *gilets jaunes*, which had started as a protest on fuel taxes but quickly evolved into a broad rebellion against a governing elite seen as remote and out of touch.

Back in the fifth century, the same kind of internal division became a characteristic feature of political discourse in the remaining territories of the Western Empire. Elite opinion was divided over how best to preserve social and economic advantage in the face of an imperial centre whose power was in decline, faced by a cocktail of increasing tax demands and the growing political reach of the barbarian confederations. Some were ready to embrace a new political order of fully independent barbarian kingdoms, whereas others, like Sidonius himself (p. 96), wanted to remain Roman at all costs. Such divisions played a substantial role in the terminal stages of Roman imperial collapse. In the modern West many separate strands of resentment can be discerned within the manifest bitterness of all the current protest and division. But, like the political divides which plagued fifth-century Rome, it has a single underlying catalyst, and its overall consequences could pose an existential threat to the nation states of the modern Western world.

HOMELANDS FOR HEROES

All states that function on the basis of political consent rely on some kind of fiscal contract: a basic set of reasons why taxpayers are willing to fund the structure within which they live. The Roman Empire, like most pre-modern states, operated with an extremely simplified version. Its state structures basically only covered defence and law with a limited amount of patronage, the latter mostly for a numerically small landowning political constituency. Roughly three-quarters of its tax revenues were spent on supporting a professional army, which protected the interests of this landowning constituency against both external and internal threats. In return, the landowners had to pay over a percentage of their agricultural surpluses and run the necessary administrative institutions. The Empire's other key centralized structure was its legal system, which again served landowning interests by defining and protecting private property and setting out a series of measures to allow its exploitation and transmission over time (by inheritance, marriage settlement and sales). The vast majority of the population were not involved in any of the state's political processes and had no say in either the rates at which taxes were levied or where they were spent. The state offered them little in the way of direct support, apart from regimes of bread and circuses to help keep the peace in a handful of major cities. Fundamentally, the mass of the peasant population had few options available to them to exercise sustained influence over the political entity within which they lived.

Large-scale revolt was not, however, a characteristic feature of Roman history and disgruntled peasants' only realistic outlet for dissent lay in low-level outlawry and brigandage. That's not to say that the course of imperial history ran smoothly: far from it. Throughout its existence, military setbacks could prompt civil wars, especially when landowning communities felt ignored or unprotected in times of danger – but these were struggles to control the system for the benefit of particular interest groups, not to break away from it entirely. Individual landowners always wanted to pay less tax, and squabbled locally to minimize their contributions, but they were broadly happy with the deal. Only when outside invasion and annexation in the fifth century undermined the Empire's ability to defend its landowners did the situation change. At that point, provincial landowners, whether they liked it or not, were forced to cut new deals with intrusive outsiders to retain some control over their physically immoveable landed estates. Once the Empire could no longer keep its end of the bargain, the contract quickly broke down, and the final unravelling of the imperial system took less than a generation as provincial landowners negotiated new relationships, wherever that option was available, with the most likely barbarian overlord within their sphere of interest (p. 96).

In contrast, modern Western states draw on much wider political bases, involving a much greater percentage of the population, and operate with a far more elaborate fiscal contract. From the second half of the nineteenth century, state structures evolved across the West to provide (in different combinations) a vast range of services to all their citizens: everything from healthcare and education to income support, to security. These services were made possible by the incomparably larger revenue surpluses that were becoming available to governments from industrialization, combined with the increased bureaucratic capacity states developed to manage them. This astonishing revolution also required major ideological shifts in understandings of what governments *should* do. The massive increase in service provision was partly a result of the higher level of demands that modern states began to make on their citizens. The chronology of these related developments is clear. Mass conscription and global conflict came first, as Britain and France struggled for world domination in the later eighteenth century and the Napoleonic war era, generating consequent demands for a political structure that would take care of citizens required to make such sacrifices.

But the advent of what would become the 'welfare state' was also a product of the fundamental ways modern industry altered the balance of power among social classes. Increasingly urbanized and highly organized within large and complex workplaces, the labouring classes acquired a degree of sustained political leverage unavailable to their rural ancestors. Medieval peasants *could* pose a momentary threat to the prevailing socio-political order, as the English king Richard II found out in 1381. In that year, a vast body of rural labourers assembled from the counties nearest London, and moved on the city in a mass revolt which claimed the lives of both the city's Lord Mayor and the Archbishop of Canterbury. To end the protests, the king had no choice but to grant them a charter of liberties. But then the protestors had to go home, because their food had run out. Once they'd dispersed, the king not only tore up the charter, but was able to send small groups of armed men round the Home Counties to deal with the ringleaders individually.

Unlike rural peasants, however, industrial workers came to the cities in large numbers, and stayed there permanently. Faced with the growing demands of the social movements that sprang up to represent this new body of humanity, and which threatened to break out into open class warfare, governments lessened the tension by mobilizing some of the profits of industrialization to build the more consensual social forms of the modern West step by step: extending the franchise, improving conditions and shortening the working week, raising wages and bettering public health. Germany's founding Chancellor Otto von Bismarck was no bleeding-heart liberal, but he knew an opportunity when he saw one, recognizing that instituting the world's first public pensions and job insurance schemes was the surest way to win votes from the Social Democrats he so loathed. By such means there gradually evolved a new type of relationship between government and people, embodied in the principle of citizenship, where both rich and poor shared a common legal status (if not always the resources to uphold it), which reached its zenith in the decades after 1945. A long period of relative political harmony was built around broad acceptance of the idea that the state *should* create 'a land fit for heroes', whose citizens would be looked after from cradle to grave, and that it was reasonable for states to exact the higher levels of taxation required to pay for it. In Britain, both Labour and the Conservatives fought the 1945 election on the basis of creating a welfare state, and such ideas – if in different combinations and to different extents – were spreading across the Western world at the time. Political dispute was limited largely to quarrelling over exactly how much tax should be paid by whom, and how exactly it should be spent, rather than any fundamental hostility towards the overall system.

This golden age of harmony and social reform, while often exaggerated to obscure the all too real divisions which remained (such as race, especially in America), has often been attributed to sound political leadership and progressive, particularly Keynesian, economics. Both undoubtedly played a role, but so too did the Western world's continued ascendancy in the global economic system. Net inflows of wealth from Europe's empires in the nineteenth century meant that governments had begun to raise living standards for the working class without having to tax the rich heavily. Manchester factories relied on sales to and cheap cotton from India, thereby inflating wages without diminishing profits. In effect, social harmony was bought by outsourcing exploitation to the colonies. In the 'provinces', including in the now-independent United States, the effect was similarly obtained by opening up new lands to European colonization and exploitation. Riots over unemployment and poverty in New York or Baltimore, which spread after the Civil War with the growth of the railways, could be defused by encouraging young men to go west and start new lives. Similar processes unfolded in Australia and Canada. And even Western countries that didn't possess their own empires could benefit from the rise of empires to the extent they were able to export into the emerging imperial system.

After World War II, as the Western Empire reached its post-colonial, confederal stage of development, prosperity peaked, and the most ambitious governmental welfare structures the world has ever seen – like Britain's National Health Service – came into existence. Political and ideological developments within Western nations play a central role in this story, but it is vitally important to understand that this extraordinary edifice was constructed on a flow of wealth from the less-developed world into the West, which provided much of the necessary revenue. All of which helps explain why the relative social and political harmony of the post-war period is now showing such strain.

WINNERS AND LOSERS

The neoliberal globalization of the 1980s and 1990s brought to the surface an underlying fragility in the relative post-war consensus. Rather than resurrecting the broad-based economic dynamism of the decades immediately after 1945, neoliberalism disproportionately restored growing prosperity to certain groups within Western societies. Whereas pretty much everyone in the West had gained one way or another from the flows of wealth from the periphery up to this point, the new economic order brought into being by globalization increased the flow of wealth mainly to particular subgroups within Western society, while simultaneously undercutting the productive livelihoods of many others. The overall effect was to generate a situation in which the primary winners and losers of the latest iteration of global economic organization were now living side by side within the same set of borders, instead of most of the losers being located, as before, at a politically safe distance overseas. In effect, the exploitation and deprivation that had been outsourced in the nineteenth and earlier twentieth centuries now came back home to the West.

The most obvious economic beneficiaries were the owners and shareholders of the firms that shifted production overseas. But, given the increasing premium on ideas and creativity in the new global economy, the group of winners also included those fortunate enough to be equipped with the kinds of skills and education – 'knowledge-capital' in the jargon of economics – to fill the higher-skilled roles the West largely retained. The newly restored profitability of globalized firms drove up share values and swelled the incomes of urban professionals who worked in these companies' offices, or who oversaw their high-end processes, like design, engineering and marketing. Moreover, with costs lowered by the move to peripheral production, inflation (that nightmare of the 1970s) fell. That in turn meant interest rates could fall, which supported house-buying and drove up property prices. This generated a boom period especially for the upper echelon of the middle class – meaning, roughly speaking, the top 10 per cent of Western society, or, in the early twenty-first century, almost anyone earning upwards of about $70,000 a year.[22] It was not just that their average earnings rose. Since they often both owned houses and were earning generous pension rights in plans that were also riding the boom in asset values, particularly in stocks and real estate, their overall standard of living improved substantially. These gains were won, however, at the expense of the less skilled and unskilled labourers who saw their previously direct participation in the process of wealth creation move overseas, and found themselves increasingly left to compete for service jobs in an economic environment that was driving down their real earnings. This trend showed up right across the West, but was most acute in the United States owing to its less developed welfare state. In the four decades after the election of Ronald Reagan, the real incomes of the bottom half of society more or less flatlined, whereas the top half saw growth – with the top 10 per cent doing best of all, enjoying an income rise of a third.[23]

Although these trends were increasingly visible in the data, late twentieth-century public discourse reassured itself that a 'new paradigm' of endless growth amid low inflation would ensure that all boats rose on this economic tide, even if left-leaning governments did sometimes qualify their optimism. In Britain, the Blair government was anxious enough to try to address the problem of so-called sink estates – increasingly alienated population clusters left out of the renewed prosperity of the 1980s and 1990s — and to devote a small fortune in public spending, much of it borrowed against supposed future income, to all levels of education in an effort to equip a bigger share of the population to participate at the top end of the rapidly globalizing economy.

Some specific policy choices also helped disguise the broader significance of these trends. Throughout the 1980s and 1990s, although average real wages barely budged across much of the Western world – in the United States, for instance, the real hourly wage currently stands roughly where it was in the mid-1970s – falling inflation kept prices low, partly obscuring losses in buying power. This was also the moment that China began flooding Western markets with cheap products (p. 124). In this context many Western governments implemented policies that eased access to credit for the less well-off. In America the federal government, using its leverage over the major agencies providing mortgage financing, lowered the collateral thresholds on loans.[24] Such measures encouraged a house-buying boom that became a self-fulfilling prophecy. As more people bought houses, prices rose, persuading these new homeowners that they were also along for the global ride – and simultaneously encouraging still more people to buy homes.

At the tail-end of the 1990s, markets were then pushed to stratospheric heights by the knock-on effects of the punishing austerity that the US government, as a condition for its help during the 1997–8 financial crisis, imposed on many peripheral governments, particularly those like Thailand and Indonesia which were at the south-east Asian epicentre of the crisis. Many economists blamed the crisis on the neoliberal opening of capital markets that Western governments had earlier prodded developing countries to adopt, since the resulting rush of capital into the periphery drove property values sky-high before they finally crashed. They thus called not for austerity but for more generous spending to stave off economic collapse. However, the Clinton administration waved them off, demanding that governments in receipt of aid slash their spending and open their markets to Western imports. The resulting austerity pushed developing countries into devastating recessions, but proved hugely beneficial for Western economies. Rich investors in peripheral countries, panicked by the resulting political instability at home, parked their money in Western bank accounts, from where it duly found its way into circulation. As the millennium drew to a close, therefore, Western investors and consumers were gorging on cheap debt, which they used to buy shares, houses, and pay for winter vacations. Politicians and policymakers, meanwhile, could still insist all was well, since the value of everyone's investments, in real estate, shares and bonds, was rising faster than their debts, making everyone richer by the day. In this broader context, it didn't matter if average wages stagnated. Everyone was apparently riding a neoliberal wave of cheap credit to greater prosperity.

The risks were always apparent for those willing to look. The whole edifice was actually operating as one vast Ponzi scheme. If, for any reason, the flow of new funds that kept pushing up house prices and the stock market began to dry up – or worse, began falling – Westerners were going to have a mountain of debt on their hands, and not enough income to pay for it. Or as Warren Buffett put it, we would only find out who was skinny-dipping when the tide went out.

It didn't take too long for that to happen. At the turn of the millennium, once the worst of the Asian financial crisis of 1997–8 passed, rich investors in developing countries began withdrawing their funds from Western accounts and bringing them back home. Coincidentally, but symbolically, this reversal in the direction of global capital flows occurred just as developing countries were launching their fightback against Western hegemony at the Seattle WTO Summit in 1999 (p. 115). The neoliberal model began to head into crisis, which the US Federal Reserve tried to alleviate by cutting interest rates, which only further inflated a housing bubble in the West. When that bubble finally burst in 2007–8 and property prices crashed, the world was staring at an economic depression.

Western governments raced to plug the holes in the dike, but the chosen solutions again both increased prevailing levels of debt and largely reinforced the new social divides created by globalization. Once more, central banks, led by the US Federal Reserve, printed trillions of new dollars, euros and pounds, which they loaned to their banks at practically zero per cent interest: the hope being that the banks would in turn then lend the money on to businesses and ordinary people. Businesses, according to this logic, would invest, expand, and thus hire workers, restarting the economy, while ordinary people would take advantage of cheap mortgage loans and credit cards to resume buying and spending. Unfortunately, while this suite of policies did avert immediate depression, it ended up exposing the widening social and political divisions that had remained largely hidden during the credit-fuelled years that had gone before. Stock markets roared back to life, New York's Dow Jones average rising some 18 per cent a year after its post-2007 crash. But new investment in productive activities proved tepid. Much of the money was used by businesses to boost executive pay and buy back their own shares instead of hiring new workers, further inflating their share values and with them year-end executive bonuses. In the decade after the Crash, American investment in new productive assets, everything from machines to software, increased only by about a half; whereas share buybacks quadrupled. Employers did resume hiring, but the established patterns of globalization continued. The new jobs tended to be service-sector and relatively low paid. All told, the rich got richer and everyone else just about got by.

In contemporary political discourse, the prevailing sense of division began to be expressed along several axes. 'Old versus young' showed up starkly in Britain's Brexit referendum results. Other debates have pitted professionals versus working people, and large cities versus town and country, or blamed 'metropolitan' and 'coastal' 'elites' for turning their backs on the ordinary folk of the heartland. Native-born versus immigrants, who were supposedly taking jobs and lowering wages, also got a plentiful airing. Some of these divides were not new – anti-immigrant discourse (not unknown even in the Roman world) has been around forever – but a clear sign that the current divisions reflected a deeper kind of structural change was visible in the emergence of new patterns of political allegiance. On the political right, in particular, a new breed of populist politicians channelled growing discontent into a supposedly anti-Establishment politics that appealed to the 'left-behind' and 'deplorables': those ignored or even derided by mainstream politicians. Such approaches flipped the traditional left-right divide, seeing workers abandon socialist and liberal parties for new right-wing movements, and played no small role in both the Brexit referendum and the rise of Donald Trump. The far right also gained power in Austria and profoundly disrupted the politics of Germany, France, Italy and Spain.

Underlying all this divisive labelling is the fundamental distinction between those who benefited from the remaking of the world economy after the new patterns of globalization, and those who did not. The generational gap *has* widened as young people, loaded with student debt and stuck with inflated housing costs, look with envy at the wealth that many older members of Western society have built up through property ownership and their pension funds. The values of both types of asset have grown astronomically over the last forty years. Someone who bought a house in Britain in the early 1960s

would, on average, have enjoyed a hundredfold return over the intervening period. In London, even owning a small terraced house would
enable someone to cash out into a life of relative luxury. A similar
transformation has affected pension funds. Between 20 and 30 per
cent of the total wealth of the Western world is now held by them,
and they have been able to boost returns for their members by taking
advantage of cheap money and increasingly shifting investments
towards the global periphery. This double change represents a shift of
potentially colossal significance. In the nineteenth and twentieth centuries, the growth of wealth in Western societies followed the growth
of income. As people's incomes rose, they set aside more of it in savings and investments. But over the last generation, the two have
become decoupled, with wealth rising faster than income (despite saving rates changing little, or even declining) – though governments still
tend to find it politically easier to tax income rather than wealth.

The divide between professional and working classes likewise
reflects the essential cleavage between those lucky enough to have
entered the job market with the necessary skills to acquire or retain
the well-paid, attractive positions which remained in the West when
production shifted elsewhere. Indeed, the kind of education – 'knowledge capital' – that is usually required to win one of these attractive
jobs often relies on parents who are sufficiently well-off to invest
heavily in their children's upbringing. When you take into account
that these same better-off families are also likely to own properties
and pension assets, Western societies are coming to be marked by an
increasing division between the better-off whose income derives primarily or substantially from the ownership of different types of
wealth, and those making their living from work. This effectively
means, of course, that the kinds of opportunity for self-advancement
and social mobility that characterized Western societies across much
of the twentieth century are disappearing fast.

In the Roman world, Roman provincial landowners, faced with
the centre's increasing inability to maintain their privileges, often
turned to negotiating with the nearest barbarian king to preserve their
landed assets. The equivalent modern elite, those benefiting from the
fruits of globalization, have likewise effectively shifted a significant
proportion of their asset portfolios to the out-sourcing centres of the

periphery. They still may own expensive properties in the inflated real estate markets of the West, but many of their assets, whether controlled directly by themselves or indirectly by pension funds, are now invested in the periphery. All told, the economic restructuring of the last forty years has seen the formation of two political constituencies within most Western societies with profoundly different economic interests. Not only has this development already generated serious division within many Western societies, but it poses a deep longer-term challenge to the whole nation-state structure which evolved in the nineteenth and twentieth centuries to become such a defining characteristic of life in the modern West.

The working structures of the Roman Empire were similarly damaged by the rise of barbarian confederations on Western soil. As the imperial centre increasingly lost control of the provinces which constituted its tax base, its capacity to maintain effective armed forces was undermined. It responded by raising tax rates for what remained of its tax base but that only increased the potential attractions of shifting allegiance to one of the barbarian confederations, and produced nowhere near enough new income to replace the overall loss in its revenues. In the end, even someone like Sidonius, who had been desperate to remain within a Roman political orbit, was eventually left with no choice but to mend his fences with the Visigothic king Euric, and it was that kind of move which marked the real end of Empire in the Roman West.

Today, globalization is generating the same kind of revenue crisis for the nation state that left the Roman West eventually unable to fulfil its fiscal contract. The shift of capital offshore has meant, in effect, that peripheral governments have been able to capture an increasing share of global income, whereas Western governments have been forced to compete for investment by keeping a lid on spending so as to keep taxes low. Moreover, the liberalization of financial markets which facilitated out-sourcing also made it easier for the top echelon of global society to move money into tax havens offshore, with roughly a tenth of global wealth – over $7 trillion – now lying beyond the reach of any government.[25]

As the divisive effects of globalization became obvious in Western societies in the late twentieth century, therefore, the flow of tax revenues available to its leaders to maintain Western living standards was already being constrained. The late Roman Empire responded to the erosion of its tax base by raising rates on what remained. The leaders of the modern West, however, were able to turn to a different solution – one of the miracle-inventions of the modern world: debt. But this may have been no more than a clever way of kicking the can down the road.

DEBT AND DISEASE

Debt, the idea of spending today but paying in the future, is as old as trade. But in the modern period, the advent of central banking – the Dutch, Swedish and English central banks coming into being in the seventeenth century – revolutionized state policy: it now became possible to reschedule payment not just into the near future but many decades hence, via thirty-year mortgages and hundred-year government bonds. Indeed, the history of the nation state is inseparable from the rise of national debt. And amid the rapid social and technological changes of the twentieth century, which were transforming the productivity of labour, borrowing against the future earnings that ultimately resulted from productive investment enabled economies to accelerate their growth.

It's not always easy to separate borrowing for productive investment, however, from borrowing to cover immediate spending. Governments often make investments to protect jobs or provide some other kind of immediate benefit – as was the case with 1970s-style nationalizations, or both Tony Blair's expansion of welfare spending against future income gains (which failed to materialize) and Boris Johnson's plans – not abandoned by his successors – to 'level up' neglected areas in the north and Midlands of Britain; plans which may or more probably will not pay for themselves. Even seemingly old-style infrastructure projects in the modern West aren't always what they seem. In 2020, Johnson announced what he called a 'Rooseveltian' investment programme. In proportionate terms, it was actually about one-thirtieth the size of the New Deal, leading the *Financial Times* to note that whereas Roosevelt built the Hoover

Dam, Johnson would be repairing a bridge in the Midlands.[26] The comparison is deeply revealing. Building a new bridge opens up new channels of trade, reducing costs and travel times, thereby generating new economic activity. Repairing a bridge just allows you to keep existing channels open, preserving the current level of activity (after, of course, the several years of longer journey times while the work is done). Similarly, when the United States alternatively experimented with a major tax cut in 2017, President Trump said it would pump rocket fuel into the economy. It didn't. Growth notched up only by 0.7 per cent in the following year, after which it fell back to its underlying rate (close to 2 per cent per year, and declining). Corporate investment barely budged, and the promised jobs boom failed to materialize, with employment growth continuing on its existing trajectory. In the end, most of the money that firms saved in taxes went towards dividends and share buybacks. This boosted share prices, further enriching a small minority of the very wealthiest Americans while doing little for the more general economy.

In reality, we live in a world in which the big economic returns which can be obtained by infrastructure spending and other types of direct government stimulus have increasingly shifted away from the West. Some economists continue to insist that this will change, that another productivity revolution to rival earlier ones like those connected to the spread of steam power or electricity will come along to restore the growth rates of old, the expected candidate for the future revolution usually being information technology. But we've been waiting a long time for that. Robert Solow famously said back in 1987 that we could see the computer age everywhere but in the productivity statistics, and that still seems to be the case.

Instead, in most Western countries productivity growth – the cash-value of what a worker produces in an hour on the job – has been on a downward curve for a long time now. After a historic boom in the mid-twentieth century, when output value per hour rose by nearly 3 per cent a year, the 1970s onwards have seen output increases per hour fall back towards their norm (which, for most of history, was nearly zero) and it is now approaching around 1 per cent a year. Where we do see large increases in worker output, they tend to be highly concentrated. The most dynamic and productive economic sectors, those in which Western countries continue to enjoy an edge, produce a bifurcated demand for labour. In high-tech industries, a relatively small percentage of the workforce is highly productive, Facebook's 60,000 employees generating nearly $90 billion in revenue in 2020, for an average of $1.5 million per annum each. They are then supported by a larger, less specialist workforce of cleaners, nannies and baristas. In other words, effective productivity gains in today's Western societies are about the few and not the many, and may do little to revolutionize the productivity of the mass of the Western workforce. So whereas debt was once a way of spending today to increase tomorrow's earnings, for most in the West it has now become a way of having things now and paying for them tomorrow.

Because the old invest-to-expand relationship has broken down, Western governments and societies have got into the habit of using debt less to build future prosperity and more to boost or sustain present standards of living. As productivity growth slowed, dragging overall income growth down with it, households and businesses kept themselves in the style to which they'd grown accustomed by taking on more debt. For a long time, governments assured them it was a safe thing to do, with repeated declarations that another productivity revolution would come along to wipe out the debts and by instituting measures, such as interest rate reductions and reduced barriers to credit, that made it ever easier to borrow.

This is all new. Although debt has become ubiquitous in Western societies, it's easy to forget that the humble credit card, that essential tool of modern life, didn't exist until the mid-twentieth century. Before then debt was generally limited to investment, in the form of businesses building plants or families buying homes, while government debts that had soared during wartime came back down afterwards. In the decades after World War II, for instance, the total ratio of private and public debt combined with GDP in the United States generally hovered around 100 per cent, a trend mirrored in other Western societies. Things really took off in the era of globalization, however, when debt was used by both governments and individuals to paper over shortfalls in revenue and worsening inequalities, or even just to maintain expectations that wealth would continue to increase.

The end result was the colossal level of debt that had built up in the West towards the end of the second decade of the twenty-first century. In 2019, Trump's tax cut pushed the national debt of the United States above 100 per cent of GDP. Once debt accumulated by ordinary citizens is added to the mix, the country's underlying debt-to-GDP ratio stood at over 300 per cent, three times the level of the post-war boom years. Britain's is similar, Italy's is worse and the *palme d'or* for fiscal imprudence goes to Japan, whose total debt-to-GDP ratio has now reached nearly five to one. This trend spreads right across the Western world. Even countries which fancy themselves frugal, like Denmark and the Netherlands, have total debt-to-GDP ratios well above 300 per cent, while even the most tight-fisted, Germany, isn't far behind at substantially over 200 per cent.

Instead of a productivity revolution riding to the rescue and bringing these debt ratios back down, however, what the West got was an unforeseen dose of exogenous shock – not in the form of hordes of Huns, but of a microscopic organism. Early in 2020, reports came out of China that a novel strain of coronavirus had emerged in the city of Wuhan. Within weeks it was spreading across the globe. By and large the initial response of Western governments was understated. But come early March 2020, when the World Health Organization labelled the outbreak a pandemic, panic erupted. Governments imposed lockdowns at home and began closing borders to international travel. Acting with record speed, most Western governments cobbled together economic rescue packages. Central banks once more opened the spigots, creating masses of new money with which they then bought both government and corporate bonds: providing the funds governments used to keep idle businesses afloat. Immediate economic depression was staved off, but, once again, the divisions within Western society worsened. Central banks drove interest rates down into the basement, in some countries taking them into negative figures – which is to say, anyone lending to the government now had to pay for the privilege. This not only encouraged firms to borrow huge amounts of money to boost their cash piles, but also encouraged investors squeezed out of bond markets by the dreadful returns to go looking elsewhere, turning to stocks, real estate and new inventions like crypto-currencies. After sharp plunges early in the year, stock markets bounced back to wipe out their losses by the summer. But across wider society, despite the rescue packages, real wages stagnated and small businesses went to the wall.

Barely any of this new borrowing was spent on the kind of investments which promised any real hope of new economic growth. So much money was pumped into stock markets on both sides of the Atlantic, and especially in America, that even technically bankrupt 'zombie' companies saw their share values rocket. In the space of a few months, Western governments increased their debt burdens by as much as 25 per cent. All told, managing the pandemic forced them to add some $17 trillion to their debts before the end of the year (the burden of public debt in Western countries generally rising by 10–20 per cent). The Western response to the Covid crisis has thus brought to the forefront of debate with a renewed urgency the key questions that were already lurking beneath the surface of globalization. Who will pay off the West's staggering levels of incurred debts, and how? And what will be the shape of Western society afterwards?

It would be hard to overestimate how much is at stake here. The western half of the Roman Empire collapsed into non-existence when the centre found itself left with insufficient funds to maintain its fiscal contract, and defend the interests of its tax-paying, tax-raising elites. The state revenue crisis unfolding in the modern West has different roots, but it doesn't take a whole lot of thought to realize that this poses a threat to what has become the characteristic state form of the modern West, one which is potentially just as existential as that which undermined the Roman West in the fifth century.

THE CENTRE CANNOT HOLD?

This is not the first time Western governments have found themselves heavily in debt. After World War II, their accumulated debts reached record levels. Today, some analysts – particularly those belonging to the school of modern monetary theory[27] – argue that now, as then, these debts will be paid off relatively painlessly through further economic growth. They reason that every hundred dollars in invested debt will ultimately yield several hundred in increased output, and the

West's current debts, just like those of the post-1945 period, will be settled within a few decades.

There are, however, some critical differences between 1945 and today. For one thing, in 1945 only about 5 per cent of the population was retired, the great productivity boom of the post-war period lay ahead, and the debts were taken on to fund basic reconstruction, leading to immediate economic expansion. Returns on investment in today's West appear unlikely to reach anything like past levels, not least because much of the recent debt – including virtually everything added during the pandemic – was taken on just to keep economies from collapsing. These debts didn't even aim to add new output; hoping to preserve what was there from disappearing, they are not likely to pay for themselves.

Second, the demands on governmental spending are only likely to increase. With the population ageing and needing more healthcare, pensions and public services – sectors that, in countries like Japan, account for up to a third of total public spending – governments will face continual strain on their budgets. Currently, between 15–20 per cent of the population in most Western countries has retired, and those figures will continue rising – by mid-century, on current trends, to something closer to the 25–30 per cent range. Nearly half of those retired will continue to be aged over seventy-five, the point at which health spending per capita generally starts to increase dramatically. Rather grimly, Western treasuries have reached the point that falling life expectancy would be considered good news, a point dramatized when in 2022 the UK Treasury reported a small windfall gain from the fact the pandemic had shortened expected lifetimes.

Third, current interest rates on governmental debt are extremely low. The US ten-year bond, for instance, which acts as a benchmark for interest rates across the American economy, rose to nearly 16 per cent in 1980 before beginning a long fall, reaching nearly zero per cent in 2020, a trend mirrored in most other developed economies. Even so, in February 2022, the British state made the largest interest payment on accrued governmental debt in its history. When interest rates began rising in Western societies in 2022, governments confronted a new problem – that the burden of interest payments would begin to eat further into their spending power. To this we can add an element that scarcely existed in a serious way after the war – namely the burden of private debt, which as we have seen has also soared over the last few decades.

If the debts won't just grow away and are in fact set to increase, along with the interest payments that have to be made on them, what options are there for Western governments, not to mention their citizens, who have to deal with this increasingly pressing financial problem?

Central banks could decide to prolong 'financial repression' indefinitely, keeping interest rates below inflation for extended periods. This was a further dimension of the policy mix following World War II, when government borrowing costs were kept below the rate of inflation, allowing the value of debt to be eaten away over time by inflation. This would be good for governments, whose tax revenues rise with inflation whereas the debt does not. If, say, Western central banks kept real interest rates – the difference between interest rates and the current rate of inflation – at minus 3 per cent (by 2022 they were double that), the value of the income from a loan to the government would effectively halve in about twenty-five years. While this might seem a clever way to postpone dealing with the problem until it eventually disappears, it would be socially disruptive. Start with all those retired voters, who have proven themselves to be a politically vigorous bloc in democratic societies, not only because their numbers are rising but because they are among the most likely to turn out on polling day. While pension funds rode the boom in asset values of the neoliberal age, with their memberships now ageing, they will increasingly need to buy government bonds, since these provide the steady income-stream someone receiving a monthly payment expects.[28] Financial repression would thus diminish the value of these income streams over time. Politicians might hope nobody notices, but someone who retired today and then spent the rest of their lives having to progressively tighten their belts would probably realize what was happening and quite likely vote accordingly.

Governments could instead try the time-honoured combination of cutting spending and/or raising taxes. But this faces two huge obstacles. The first is that the costs embedded in the existing Western fiscal contract will only push spending upwards. Even before the pandemic, which revealed how degraded Britain's National Health Service had become after a decade of austerity, it was broadly accepted that health spending required an increase of 4 per cent each year just to keep up with rising demand and the additional costs of rising technological possibility. And that's taking no account of increasing pension spending; in 2022 the British prime minister admitted that growth of 1 or 2 per cent would not be enough to pay for the NHS over the long term. It's one thing to ask citizens to pay taxes for improved services, something they are often happy to do. It's another to ask them to pay taxes to cover the costs of services already rendered – paid for in the past with debt – especially if these are services from which they may never benefit.

Western governments currently raise most of their revenue from taxes on income and consumption. Consumption taxes, such as sales taxes and VAT, raise prices, while income taxes fall heavily on the working population. As things stand, with the ageing population growing by the year in Western countries, the average worker already shares the burden of supporting one pensioner with one other active member of the labour force. Between now and mid-century that figure will move inexorably closer to one-to-one. In other words, the tax burden on younger, working-age people is already set to rise, and saddling them with the extra burden of the combined debts of globalization and the coronavirus pandemic would mean considerable increases on top. In Britain, for instance, university graduates entering the workforce can be expected to now lose as much as half their monthly income to taxes. This leads to the second big problem with raising taxes to pay debt. When taxes go up but public services don't follow, the risk is that the fiscal contract comes to be perceived as broken. The Roman case shows what can happen in that situation.

The least-worst policy mix for fixing the West's debt problem is still not going to be easy. In all likelihood it will consist of continued interest-rate suppression for those economies that can get away with it, combined with various cocktails of tax hikes and service cuts. Trying to ignore these financial constraints will lead to disastrous economic outcomes via ever-increasing interest rates, as Britain's abortive 'mini-budget' of autumn 2022 revealed. Getting the latter combination right – in a general context of ageing populations and low growth – will be particularly difficult. Reduce services too far, and you spark increased social unrest and start to hollow out the vital functions of the state. In the late twentieth century, some developing countries were faced with similar debt problems, and had to raise taxes and tighten spending, both on a substantial scale and often with little Western sympathy – even, in the case of the austerity imposed by the Clinton administration in the wake of the Asian Crisis, finding themselves plunged into crisis just as the West was celebrating its maximum prosperity. The experience in many of these countries is revealing of the potential problems ahead for the West. In many cases, much of the working population effectively withdrew from the tax net. At the bottom end, small contractors conducted all their business in cash, importers bribed underpaid customs officers not to tax their imports, and the ultra-rich hid their wealth in Swiss bank accounts, resulting in a vicious downward spiral: declining revenues forced further reductions in government services.

In the worst-hit countries, the austerity packages of the late twentieth century broke the existing fiscal contract, citizens at the top and bottom opted out of the existing political structure, and power was effectively redistributed, sometimes ending up in some very undesirable hands. In inner-city communities controlled by drug gangs in Jamaica and Brazil, in the regions of Mexico held by the cartels, in the borderlands of Pakistan or much of Afghanistan where the Taliban were active, states-within-states were able to establish themselves. This might seem very far away, but we've already started to see early manifestations of this showing up in the West – not merely in the fact that some depressed areas in many Western cities are virtual gang fiefdoms, but also in the state's growing incapacity to keep its side of the bargain. In Britain, for instance, budget cuts to police and court systems have resulted in a situation where barely one rape in a hundred now ends up being punished: in effect, decriminalization by stealth. As people are forced to pay more in taxes to pay off past debts, but governments offer less in return, a point may well come when citizens begin to wonder what they are getting in return for their tax compliance. And given the impact on tax revenues of both 'tax morale' – the belief that you get something for your taxes, which makes people willing to report their incomes and pay their taxes honestly – and the diminishing effectiveness of tax-collection agencies, which are themselves often cutback-targets for penny-pinching governments, it is not unreasonable to ponder a future in which more and more people find ways to slip out of the tax net – just like the provincial elites of fifth-century Rome – heralding the collapse of the entire system.

Such a future – of increasing political fragmentation, rising instability, waning democracy and respect for the law and human rights, eroding public services and declining living standards – may await the West. But it doesn't have to.

Conclusion
Death of the Empire?

As spring turned to summer in AD 468, Constantinople came once more to the defence of the Roman West. The current Western emperor, Anthemius, was an Eastern appointee, who had come from Constantinople a year earlier with promises of serious military assistance. The Eastern Emperor, Leo I, was as good as his word. The East's intervention took the form of a vast armada of 1,100 ships and a combined force of 50,000 soldiers and sailors, which cost over 120,000 pounds weight in gold. The expedition's destination was the North African kingdom of the Vandal-Alan confederation, its central aim to eliminate one of the new confederations unintentionally set loose by the Huns on Roman soil, and return the richest provinces of the West to imperial control.

Not only would a successful outcome have reinvigorated the West Roman centre by increasing its revenue streams, but it would also have called at least a temporary halt to another dangerous phenomenon: the growing tendency for provincial Roman landowners to transfer their political allegiance from the imperial centre to one or other of the new barbarian confederations in their midst. Even before 468, Anthemius had been running a charm offensive north of the Alps trying to win back the allegiance of Gallic elites who had been moving into the political orbit of Visigothic and Burgundian kings. Victory in North Africa, with the promise of increased revenues, and hence greater military potency, would make it all the easier for Anthemius to convince dithering Western elites that continued loyalty to Rome was the best policy for the foreseeable future.

Unfortunately for Anthemius, the expedition ended in disaster. When hostile winds pinned its ships against a rocky shoreline, the

Vandals were able to launch a series of devastating attacks using fire-ships, and that was that. But, if by then too late to revive the Western Empire (which no longer existed), a later Constantinopolitan expedi-tion did succeed in destroying the Vandal kingdom in 532–3. So the task was not inherently impossible, and had its earlier counterpart enjoyed better fortune, there was a real chance to haul the West back from the brink. It would not have been the Western Empire of old. The destruction of the Vandal-Alans would still have left two power-ful barbarian confederations established on significant chunks of the Empire's former tax base, Britain was lost, and Frankish groups were encroaching across the Rhine. But the Visigoths and Burgundians would have had to accept the hegemony of an imperial centre whose status as the most powerful military and political force within their orbit would have been decisively restored, and wavering provincial elites would have rallied (more and less willingly) to their traditional loyalties. The end result might have been more of a federation under Roman imperial leadership than a straightforward Empire, and its subsequent politics would have been complex. All the same, as late as 468, there was still a real opportunity to breathe new life into a revised form of the West Roman Empire.

As this book comes to its conclusion, the modern West doesn't yet find itself in the 'last chance saloon' that faced the Roman West in the late 460s. The constituent nations of the modern Western Empire still retain control of plentiful revenues, even if these have declined a long way in relative terms from their apogee at the end of the last millen-nium. All the same, our sustained comparison with the rise and fall of the Roman Empire makes two points crystal clear. First, like ancient Rome, the modern Western Empire is facing a crisis of its own making, the operations of its own structures having stimulated the rise (finally) of a real superpower peer competitor, and assertive new powers in what had been the West's own imperial periphery. The rise of these new entities, matching what happened in the Roman world in the fourth and fifth centuries, has in turn generated serious divides within the Western imperial system at two levels, as rival Western leaders quarrel over how best to respond to this new post-imperial world order, where unprecedented prosperity for some has come to rely on the erosion of living standards for many others.

But if the West does not yet stand at a crux moment equivalent to the late 460s, it does find itself in some approximation to the situation faced by Roman leaders a few decades before, in the earlier fifth century. Like Rome, it is facing financial problems that are severe enough to threaten the entire fiscal contract on which its existing social order is based; unlike Rome, the modern West will not have the option of recolonizing some foreign breadbaskets to replenish its resource base. The kind of revenue collapse that followed the loss of North Africa has not yet occurred, though to some extent this is because a tool that was not available to Rome's rulers, debt, has allowed both governments and citizens to borrow against future revenues, which really just means that the impending revenue crisis has been postponed. Even so, the rise of a peer superpower competitor, in the form of China, is a permanent fact of life, as is the emergence of a series of powerful new entities in the old imperial periphery. If total imperial collapse remained just about reversible for ancient Rome at an even later stage, the current trajectory towards potential collapse is certainly reversible for the modern West, therefore, so long as it accepts that it cannot (and should not) attempt to restore the old colonial order of world domination.

Responding positively to the passing of that old order to achieve the best available outcome, however, will require a series of difficult adjustments beyond even those already made. At home, there will need to be a much more honest debate about the role of immigration in the context of Western populations which will continue to age and birth rates that are showing no signs of rebounding, creating ever increasing rates of social dependency. Abroad, it will be necessary to treat with much greater sympathy and equality those emerging powers that share important cultural and institutional legacies with the old Western powers, if there is going to be any real chance of building a new coalition which will be powerful enough to engage with China on properly equal terms. These are not such easy messages to sell to Western electorates as 'immigrants are taking our jobs' or the demonstrably mythical claim that acting alone – putting America, or Britain, or Poland 'first' – will enable any single Western nation to get better trading terms from China, or India for that matter, than acting as a bloc.

If a new generation of Western leaders and their electorates can rise to these challenges and follow through on current attempts to cast off colonial legacies at home, while seizing the opportunities for building the broader, more inclusive international alliances that recent responses to the Russian invasion of Ukraine have proven possible (p. 132), the unavoidable end of the old Western Empire can still generate an extremely positive set of outcomes: and not just in the West. Recast for a properly post-colonial era, the bedrock institutions of the socially integrated Western nation state – a rule of law that seeks to protect all interests, properly accountable political elites, a free press, and efficient, impartial public institutions – offer a better quality of life to a much wider range of citizens than any competing state form. Institutions do not exist in a vacuum, however, nor can they be artificially maintained. Even if their worth is generally recognized, they still rest on economic and political balances of power. Get the response to debt wrong, and fail to evolve the fiscal contract in a way that keeps enough people on board, and the West could soon be faced with the death of the nation, and its replacement with alternative, much less inclusive political structures.

In the past, when domestic political stability was threatened, governments in Western societies were able to release pressure by out-sourcing exploitation to the periphery. Today, that option is gone: they can only exploit their fellow citizens. If Western countries are to reduce their internal tensions, therefore, it seems inescapable that the better-off citizens, particularly the top 10 per cent who benefited the most from the globalization in the last few decades, will have to contribute more resources to build a new type of functioning social-political model, in the absence now of large flows of wealth from abroad. The Covid-19 pandemic, which required everyone to make sacrifices for the good of society's most vulnerable minority, and generated greater recognition of the overall social and economic contributions of less well-paid 'essential' workers, started a lively discussion of the sorts of policies that might be used to help rebuild social cohesion in the West. For any of these to work, however, Western societies will have to do a lot more than go out on the street to clap. Possible elements of a new fiscal contract include debt jubilees (especially on student debt), a universal basic income that guaranteed everyone a more generous minimum standard of living, policies to increase home-building so as to widen access to properly affordable housing and perhaps a shift towards larger taxes on wealth as opposed to income. Again, this wouldn't be easy, not least because the wealthy have a lot of influence within the political system. But, in addition to the fact that wealth taxes target those most able to pay, they can also help re-energize the economy: by rewarding those who invest their wealth to create new income and penalizing those who try only to accumulate more wealth, whether in land speculation or superyachts, wealth taxes can steer money towards more productive uses. Such changes probably also need to be accompanied, at least in some countries, with measures to reduce insecure employment by strengthening lax labour laws, of the sort that in 2022 enabled a British ferry operator to replace its workforce with cheaper employees by just paying the maximum fine it could be charged for illegally firing them overnight, then writing it off as a business expense. Alongside more secure employment, decent minimum wages, free tuition and generous job-retraining schemes to afford the unemployed decent incomes while retooling for a changing job market, this would not only build greater social cohesion but arguably also more productive businesses (a model not unlike the existing Scandinavian one).

Rebalancing the fiscal contract to reduce current trajectories towards social division will also need more, not less, international cooperation. An excellent place to start would be international tax treaties to clamp down on tax avoidance in offshore havens, estimated now to be sheltering over $7 trillion of oligarch wealth, and to reduce 'tax arbitrage', whereby multinational corporations and the rich create elaborate structures or go looking for low-tax countries in which to shelter their wealth and income, making it difficult for their home countries to find and tax them. Some of this is already happening. It's been estimated that the 2021 OECD international statement on a global minimum tax, whereby 130 countries agreed to set corporate tax rates no lower than 15 per cent, could alone provide the world's governments with an additional $150 billion of income each year.

International treaties on greenhouse-gas reduction and a Green New Deal could also prevent a race to the bottom on carbon emissions, further ensuring younger generations a liveable future. These could be combined with a global regime of carbon taxes, especially if coupled to a dividend scheme that distributed the receipts of such a carbon tax to the general population. It might then win more support among those who have often felt themselves the losers from environmental policies: the working class. By imposing costs on those who pollute most, the rich, while distributing the dividends equally, such a scheme would appropriately reward people at the lower end of the global income scale. Finally, Western countries will surely have to reform their pension systems to restore their long-term viability – postponing retirement ages, for instance, as an alternative to reducing payment levels – since when they were created nobody anticipated an era in which people might spend as much time in retirement as they had working.

None of these necessary choices will be simple to achieve. But whatever happens, the West simply can't ever make itself great again in nineteenth- and twentieth-century terms. The fundamental structures of the world economy have shifted in too profound a fashion for that ever to be possible, and some of its leaders need to stop pretending that this can be otherwise. Nor, if there's going to be any honesty at all about the degree of force and exploitation on which that modern Western Empire was originally constructed, should anyone mourn its passing. The citizens of the rising periphery would be far more likely to buy into a new world order if their material progress was no longer seen as a threat, but was welcomed and encouraged. The more shameful elements of the colonial past would then be less likely to obscure the idea that Western society eventually found its way through internal conflict to a consensual model of socio-political organization which offered more, to more of its citizens, than any rival system: not just in terms of economic prosperity but individual liberties and the political and legal rights that are easily taken for granted, but which have been so rare throughout most of human history.

If the citizens of Western countries are able to grasp the key challenges that lie ahead, resolving inevitably divisive arguments democratically in ways that give the wider citizenry a sense of inclusion and fairness, and particularly if they can do so in ways that allow the citizens of rising peripheral states to believe that they, too, are being offered a stake in a more equal future within a broader system based on the same shared values, the gains are potentially colossal. Not only would the form of the Western nation state – originally built on leveraged wealth flows from the rest of the planet – have managed to negotiate a moment of potentially existential crisis, but it would have generated a post-colonial legacy of real greatness, of which its citizens could be genuinely proud.

Notes

1. On the very fringes of this part of the political spectrum, there have been attempts to identify a 'dark conspiracy' to replace the populations of the West with immigrants from the periphery. Replacement Theory, as it calls itself, traces its origins to a 1973 dystopian novel (Jean Raspail, *Le camp des saints*), but with more than a nod to Enoch Powell's 1968 'Rivers of Blood' speech. It has partly moved from some very murky political fringes (having motivated some terrorist attacks) into slightly more mainstream circles, having turned up in the speeches of Hungary's Viktor Orbán and Italy's Matteo Salvini, whilst running through France's yellow-vest (*gilets jaunes*) movement.
2. Flavius Stilicho was born on Roman territory but his father was a Vandal immigrant. When opportunity arose nine years later, his rivals launched a bloody coup d'état in which Stilicho was summarily executed along with his children.
3. For a certain type of modern intellectual, who likes to cite Roman history to support their claim that liberal regimes produce more dynamic economies, the uncomfortable fact facing the Acemoglu-Robinson thesis is that the Roman Empire thrived *after* it abandoned republicanism.
4. Even today, the bulk of the US economy's output is consumed at home, and of its external trade, Canada and Mexico account for half; the patterns, reaching back in time, operating in periods of British, French, or Dutch domination, were not that different.
5. By this date, Constantinople was the main destination of similar exports from Egypt and Rome's Near Eastern provinces.
6. The same kinds of stories could be told of many elite individuals from the eastern half of the Empire. Their education was completed in Greek, but transmitted exactly the same ideological messages, and similarly prepared them, by the fourth century, to flourish in the structures of Empire.

7. Latin America occupied an anomalous position in the Western imperial system. Some of the original Spanish and Portuguese colonies did see large-scale European settlement, but even after winning independence at the start of the nineteenth century they never, unlike Britain's White dominions, rose to full provincial status within the developing Western imperial system. Like Spain and Portugal themselves, these colonies were dominated by the agriculturally generated wealth of an elite estate-owning class. It was these local landowners who led the independence movements, and afterwards they had little interest in overturning the economic model which had established their pre-eminence. As a result, Latin American elites remained outside the emergent culture of Western capitalism, with its increasing focus on markets, individual liberty and democracy, and the territories they dominated at best operated within the inner periphery of the emerging imperial system.

8. '$22,020,700,446 Gold Held by Treasury; About 80% of Monetary Stock of World in This Country', *New York Times*, 7 January 1941 (https://www.nytimes.com/1941/01/07/archives/22020700446-gold-held-by-treasury-about-80-of-monetary-stock-of.html)

9. Several Latin American countries and a few independent states from the periphery, like Iraq and China, attended the conference, though their impact on the final agreement proved limited.

10. The pound sterling was the world's principal reserve currency in 1945, but over the next few decades it was steadily replaced by the US dollar, and today some three-fifths of the world's foreign-exchange reserves are banked in the US (Barry Eichengreen, Livia Chițu and Arnaud Mehl, *Stability or Upheaval? The Currency Composition of International Reserves in the Long Run*, European Central Bank Working Paper Series #1715, August 2014: https://www.ecb.europa.eu/pub/pdf/scpwps/ecbwp1715.pdf.

11. The Treasury was not actually producing physical money. In effect, banks were merely instructed to credit a client's account, using dollar amounts which could in theory be redeemed for gold.

12. The 1974 CIA document assessing Soviet support for Allende is devastating in its candour, its title being simply 'The Soviets Abandon Allende'. https://www.cia.gov/library/readingroom/docs/DOC_0000307740.pdf.

13. European barbarians did defeat and kill the brief-lived Emperor Decius, but he commanded the resources of only a small part of the Empire, and his defeat was not on the kind of scale regularly administered by the Persians.

14. The other basic possibility is that the arrival of the Huns was driven by an ongoing political revolution in the steppe world towards larger empires; the two lines of explanation are not mutually exclusive.

15. The second-century, so-called Marcomannic Wars, which eventually generated the victories Marcus Aurelius celebrated on his column in Rome, had similar origins.

16. It is a general pattern in the medieval period – echoed by the Avars in the sixth century and the Magyars in the ninth – that intrusive nomads first occupy territory north of the Black Sea, and then make a subsequent secondary move westwards to the Great Hungarian Plain.

17. Its effects are visible in the *Notitia Dignitatum*, a military listing of the Eastern army dating to 395, in which sixteen units of heavy infantry can be shown to be 'missing'; that is, they had not been reformed in the intervening two decades.

18. Archaeological evidence suggests that the resulting gaps on the frontier were filled by hiring barbarian auxiliaries from beyond the frontier.

19. The Burgundians had been settled on Roman soil in the late 430s after taking a beating from the Huns; they were clearly not as powerful as the Visigothic confederation.

20. Syagrius and Leo of Narbonne were advising the Burgundian and Visigothic kings respectively; a Praetorian Prefect of Gaul called Arvandus and a deputy Prefect ('vicar') called Seronatus were both convicted of treason for encouraging neighbouring kings to increase the area of Gaul under their control.

21. In terms of their DNA, everyone of European descent is the product (if in slightly different ratios in different places) of an intermingling of three distinct population groups from the distant past: the hunter-gatherers who first repopulated the continent after the last Ice Age; an immigration of Near Eastern farmers who spread across the landscape from around 4,000 BC; and a further pulse of population from the Eurasian steppe who arrived a thousand years after that.

22. It often surprises people who think of themselves as middle or even working class (which happens with some professionals who belong to unions) to learn that they are in the richest 1 per cent of people on the planet, since most of the people they know are like them. But this reveals our (conscious or unconscious) biases in the way we socialize, or what is known as assortative mixing. At one time, marrying across classes mitigated this effect, but recent decades have seen an increase in assortative mating among the most well-off, which appears to be further distancing the top tenth from the rest of society.

23. https://ourworldindata.org/grapher/disposable-household-income-by-income-decile-absolute?time=1979..latest&country=~USA.
24. The Federal National Mortgage Association and the Federal Home Loan Mortgage Corporation, colloquially known as Fannie Mae and Freddie Mac respectively.
25. https://www.project-syndicate.org/commentary/western-sanctions-russia-oligarch-dark-money-by-daron-acemoglu-2022-03.
26. George Parker and Chris Giles, 'Johnson seeks to channel FDR in push for UK revival', 29 June 2020: https://www.ft.com/content/f708ac9b-7efe-4b54-a119-ca898ad71bfa.
27. Admittedly, some economists wonder what is so modern about it, finding it to be very similar to old-fashioned Keynesianism, and with even deeper roots in early twentieth-century German 'chartalist' theories of money.
28. As the members of a pension plan near retirement age, fund managers need to move more of their portfolio into secure investments like government bonds: they can't take the chance of investing in a potentially lucrative business venture if there's a risk the investment might fail, something that can get smoothed out by a fund manager investing for the long term but isn't an option when clients expect a regular payment each month.

Further Reading

INTRODUCTION

Edward Gibbon's masterpiece is available in full or abridged form, published by Penguin. Peter Heather's thinking about the first millennium is set out in full, with scholarly apparatus, in *Empires and Barbarians: Migration, Development, and the Birth of Europe* (London, 2009). John Rapley got to thinking about contemporary globalization and the deep cycles of rising and falling regimes in *Globalization and Inequality* (Boulder, Lynne Rienner, 2004), thereby starting a conversation with Peter Heather on the parallels between ancient and modern.

1. PARTY LIKE IT'S 399

All of Claudian's poetry can be read in the translation (with facing Latin text if you're interested) of Maurice Platnauer, *The Works of Claudian*, Loeb (London, 1922); the court at which he was working is brilliantly evoked by Alan Cameron, *Claudian: Poetry and Propaganda at the Court of Honorius* (Oxford, 1970). A classic account of the old orthodoxy of late Roman economic collapse is M. Rostovtzeff, *The Social and Economic History of the Roman Empire*, 2nd edn, rev. P. Fraser (Oxford, 1957).

The archaeologist of late Roman Syria is G. Tchalenko, *Villages antiques de la Syrie du Nord* (Paris, 1953–8), and Bryan Ward Perkins, *The Fall of Rome and the End of Civilisation* (Oxford, 2005), eloquently summarizes the subsequent evidence of late-Roman economic prosperity. The many works of Peter Brown – but see especially *The Rise of Western Christendom*, rev. 3rd edn (Oxford, 2013) – offer a brilliant pathway into the cultural efflorescence of the late Empire and beyond. The ex-British civil servant's report into the structures of its government can be found in A.H.M

Jones, *The Later Roman Empire: A Social Economic and Administrative Survey*, 3 vols (Oxford, 1964).

Roman parallels have a long lineage among modern historians, with some of the classics that still prove popular with general audiences, for better or worse, being Arnold Toynbee's *A Study of History* and Osvald Spengler's *Decline of the West*. Contemporary commentators, especially Americans or Europeans on the political right, have been particularly taken with the idea of civilization's collapse and the onslaught of barbarism, though much of it is sensationalist or poorly documented. But one seminal essay that – again, for better or worse – influenced foreign-policy thought in recent times was Robert Kaplan's 'The Coming Anarchy', which originated as an essay in the *Atlantic* (1994) and was later turned into a book (New York, 2000).

Data on contemporary world economies comes from the World Bank's *World Development Indicators*, which is one of the more authoritative and accessible databases available. The standard source for historical estimates of gross domestic product and per capita incomes through history are in the database compiled by Angus Maddison and which is now kept at https://www.rug.nl/ggdc/historicaldevelopment/maddison/releases/maddison-project-database-2020?lang=en.

2. EMPIRE AND ENRICHMENT

Ausonius' *Mosella* is translated (again with facing Latin text) by H. G. Evelyn White, *The Works of Ausonius*, Loeb, vol. 2 (London, 1961), who conveniently follows it with Symmachus' waspish response. The broader cultural evolution which produced both of them is brilliantly evoked by a combination of G. Woolf, *Becoming Roman: The Origins of Provincial Civilization in Gaul* (Cambridge, 1988), and R. A. Kaster, *Guardians of Language: The Grammarian and Society in Late Antiquity* (Berkeley, 1988). The best study of the court world in which they both operated is J. F. Matthews, *Western Aristocracies and Imperial Court A.D. 364–425* (Oxford, 1975). The exciting results produced by the late twentieth-century archaeological surveys are summarized by, among others, T. Lewitt, *Agricultural Production in the Roman Economy A.D. 200–400* (Oxford, 1991), with further reflections in C. Wickham, *Framing the early Middle Ages: Europe and the Mediterranean 400–800* (Oxford, 2005). The fourth-century commentator on Rome's political irrelevance is Themistius, in his fourth oration (for the Eastern Emperor Constantius II), which can be read translated in full in P. J. Heather and D. Moncur, *Politics, Philosophy, and Empire in the Fourth Century: Select Orations of Themistius*, Translated Texts for Historians (Liverpool, 2001).

The origins of modern capitalism remain a topic of considerable debate, to say nothing of the general curiosity they elicit in the apparent enigma of its origins (as we know it) in Europe. In *Guns, Germs and Steel: The Fates of Human Societies* (New York, 1997), Jared Diamond produced a much-discussed argument that credited capitalism's origins and expansion to environmental factors. To environmental factors Eric Jones added political ones in *The European Miracle: Environments, Economies and Geopolitics in the History of Europe and Asia* (Cambridge, 1981), a book which can be read fruitfully in tandem with Justin Yifu Lin's discussion of why capitalism did *not* originate in imperial China; in 'The Needham Puzzle: Why the Industrial Revolution Did Not Originate in China', *Economic Development and Cultural Change*, vol. 43, no. 2 (January 1995), pp. 269–92, he makes the interesting argument that the Chinese civil-service examination system encouraged ambitious young men out of industry and into bureaucracy. But perhaps the most influential synthesis of the institutional origins of capitalism currently remains Daron Acemoglu and James Robinson, *Why Nations Fail* (New York, 2012). As for early Italian capitalism, a good case study is offered in Frederic C. Lane's *Venice: A Maritime Republic* (Baltimore, 1973). The Vanderbilt family history can be reconstructed using the database https://longislandsurnames.com, and a good book on the great European migration that straddled the turn of the twentieth century is Tara Zahra, *The Great Departure: Mass Migration from Eastern Europe and the Making of the Free World* (New York, 2016).

3. EAST OF THE RHINE, NORTH OF THE DANUBE

On the establishment of Rome's frontier line and the economic development which followed in the non-Roman world, see P. J. Heather, *Empires and Barbarians: Migration, Development, and the Birth of Europe* (London, 2009), esp. ch. 2, drawing upon a wealth of archaeological research and analysis: not least Lotte Hedeager's wonderful *Iron-Age Societies: From Tribe to State in Northern Europe, 500 BC to AD 700*, trans. J. Hines (Oxford, 1992). A good introduction to the world of 'outer' Europe left untouched by Rome's rise (and fall) is P. M. Dolukhanov, *The Early Slavs: Eastern Europe from the initial Settlement to the Kievan Rus* (Harlow, 1996). The archaeological evidence for the fourth-century Tervingi is summarized in P. J. Heather and J. F. Matthews, *The Goths in the Fourth Century*, Translated Texts for Historians (Liverpool, 1991), ch. 2. On the ancient amber routes, see, for instance, A. Spekke, *The Ancient Amber Routes and the Geographical Discovery of the Eastern Baltic* (Chicago, 1976).

The life story of Jamsetji Tata can be found in F. R. Harris, *Jamsetji Nusserwanji Tata: A Chronicle of His Life* (Bombay, 1958), which can be set against S.M. Rutnagar's study of the Bombay business community of Tata's time, *The Bombay Cotton Mills: A Review of the Progress of the Textile Industry in Bombay from 1850 to 1926 and the Present Constitution, Management and Financial Position of the Spinning and Weaving Factories* (Bombay, 1927). The evolution of the contemporary global periphery is discussed in John Rapley, *Understanding Development: Theory and Practice in the Third World*, 3rd edn (Boulder, 2006), while a more fine-grained look at the development of colonial capitalism can be found in John Rapley, *Ivoirien Capitalism: African Entrepreneurs in Côte d'Ivoire* (Boulder, 1993). For a fascinating insight into how thin the layer of colonialism was in the outer periphery, the diaries of the French colonial administrator Robert Delavignette, *Freedom and Authority in French West Africa* (London, 1950), offer a very readable volume. Similarly, for India, Angus Maddison's *Class Structure and Economic Growth: India and Pakistan since the Moghuls* (London, 1971) reveals the degree to which British administration relied almost entirely on local agents.

4. THE POWER OF MONEY

The histories of Chnodomarius and Macrianus are recounted by the Roman historian Ammianus Marcellinus, translated in full (with facing Latin text) by J. C. Rolfe, *Ammianus Marcellinus*, Loeb (London, 1935–9); the otherwise excellent Penguin Classics translation unfortunately omits some of the chapters relating to Macrianus. John Drinkwater, *The Alamanni and Rome 213–496* (Oxford, 2007), is always worth reading, but tries too hard – against the run of a great deal of evidence – to turn the Alamanni into no kind of threat whatsoever: P. J. Heather 'The Gallic War of Julian Caesar', in Hans-Ulrich Wiemer and S. Rebenich (ed.), *A Companion to Julian the Apostate* (Brill, 2020). On the Gothic confederation of the Tervingi, see, P. J. Heather, *Goths and Romans 332–489* (Oxford, 1991). Dennis Green, *Language and History in the Early Germanic World* (Cambridge, 1998), discusses the linguistic evidence for the militarization of leadership in the

Germanic-speaking world. Lotte Hedeager again (see further reading for Ch. 3), on the astonishing weapons' deposits from the late Roman period.

The political awakening of the Indian business class, and its gradual warming to the nationalist movement, is discussed in Claude Markovits, *Indian Business and Nationalist Politics, 1931–1939* (Cambridge University Press, 1985), p. 32. The broad movement of decolonization and the emergence of what came to be called the Third World is detailed in John Rapley, *Understanding Development: Theory and Practice in the Third World* (Boulder, 2006). Benn Steil provides an entertaining look at the creation of the post-war Bretton Woods system, revolving around the debate between its two great architects, in *The Battle of Bretton Woods: John Maynard Keynes, Harry Dexter White, and the Making of a New World Order* (Princeton, 2013), while its full elaboration can be found in ch. 12 of John Rapley, *Twilight of the Money Gods* (London, 2017). The rapid decline of the pound sterling as the world's reserve currency thereafter, and the emergence of the global dollar order, is detailed in Barry Eichengreen, Livia Chiţu and Arnaud Mehl, *Stability or Upheaval? The Currency Composition of International Reserves in the Long Run*, European Central Bank Working Paper Series #1715, August 2014. Finally, amid all the literature on the Chilean coup, there is no better place to start than the CIA memorandum titled simply 'The Soviets Abandon Allende'. It can be accessed at https://www.cia.gov/library/readingroom/docs/DOC_0000307740.pdf.

5. THINGS FALL APART

Peter Heather's views on the end of the West Roman imperial system are set out in more detail in *The Fall of the Roman Empire: A New History of Rome and the Barbarians* (London, 2005). Alternative constructions placing less weight on the barbarian element (but not denying it) can be found in, for example, Walter Goffart, 'Rome, Constantinople, and the Barbarians in Late Antiquity', *American Historical Review* 76 (1981), 275–306; Guy Halsall, *Barbarian Migrations and the Roman West 376–568* (Cambridge, 2007); and Michael Kulikowski, *Imperial Tragedy: From Constantine's Empire to the Destruction of Roman Italy (AD 363–568)* (London, 2019). On the geo-strategic shifts involved in the recentring of Empire to northern Europe, see Peter Heather, *Empires & Barbarians: Migration, Development and the Creation of Europe* (London, 2009), with Chris Wickham, *Framing the Early Middle Ages: Europe and the Mediterranean 400–800* (Oxford,

2005). The best account now of the wars with Persia and rise of Islam which reduced Eastern Rome to Byzantium is James Howard-Johnston, *The Last Great War of Antiquity* (Oxford, 2021), with Mark Whittow, *The Making of Orthodox Byzantium, 600–1025* (London, 1996), and John Haldon, *Byzantium in the Seventh Century: The Transformation of a Culture* (Cambridge, 1990). The letters of Sidonius Apollinaris can be read in the translation (with facing Latin) of W. B. Anderson, *Sidonius Apollinaris Poems & Letters*, Loeb (London, 1936–65).

6. BARBARIAN INVASIONS

An excellent introduction to older views of the Anglo-Saxon take-over of southern Britain, and why and how they need to be revised, is Simon Esmonde-Cleary, *The Ending of Roman Britain* (London, 1989, but multiple editions). Peter Heather, *Empires & Barbarians: Migration, Development and the Creation of Europe* (London, 2009), ch. 6, provides a fuller narrative reconstruction. On the drastic simplification of post-Roman southern British material culture, see Bryan Ward Perkins, *The Fall of Rome and the End of Civilization* (Oxford, 2005), and Ellen Swift, *The End of the Western Roman Empire: An Archaeological Investigation* (Stroud, 2000). The various essays in P. Porena and Y. Rivière (eds.), *Expropriations et confiscations dans les royaumes barbares: une approche régionale* (Rome, 2012), provide an important corrective to the rose-tinted views of Walter Goffart, *Barbarians and Romans AD 418–584: The Techniques of Accommodation* (Princeton, 1980), on the realities of barbarian land-grabbing.

The 'great replacement' conspiracy theory that has gained so much on the far right finds its origins in a 2011 French book of that title by Renaud Camus, though its earliest inspiration came in a 1973 dystopian novel – also by a French author, Jean Raspail – that was translated into English as *The Camp of the Saints*. A handy data sheet on the current demography of the OECD countries is available at https://www.oecd.org/els/family/47710686.pdf. There is a very large literature which assesses the economic impact of both illegal and legal immigration in Western societies, but a few helpful starting points are Florence Jaumotte, Ksenia Koloskova, and Sweta C. Saxena, *Impact of Migration on Income Levels in Advanced Economies* (Washington, DC, 2016), Gordon H. Hanson, *The Economic Logic of Illegal Immigration* (New York, 2007), and David K. Androff et al., 'Fear vs. Facts: Examining the Economic Impact of Undocumented Immigrants in the U.S.', *Journal of Sociology and Social Welfare* 39,

4 (December 2012). Finally, of the very large literature on the decline of labour productivity in Western societies, perhaps the most authoritative (if US-focused) remains Robert J. Gordon's *The Rise and Fall of American Growth* (Princeton, 2016), though a short useful companion to that is Tyler Cowen's *The Great Stagnation* (New York, 2011).

7. POWER AND THE PERIPHERY

The effects of progressive losses of territorial tax base on the Western Roman imperial system are examined in Heather, *The Fall of the Roman Empire*, ch. 4 and following. On Eastern Rome's destructive world war with Sasanian Persia, see Howard-Johnston, *The Last Great War*, with, among many possibilities, Hugh Kennedy's excellent *The Great Arab Conquests: How the Spread of Islam Changed the World We Live In* (London, 2007), on the era of Islamic expansion it ushered in. Peter Brown's *The Rise of Western Christendom*, 3rd edn (Oxford, 2013), is a wonderful entry point into the transmission of elements of classical Roman culture into the post-Roman west.

The rise and spread of neoliberalism is discussed at length in John Rapley, *Globalization and Inequality: Neoliberalism's Downward Spiral* (Boulder, 2004), while its impact in the developing world is given extensive coverage in Rapley, *Understanding Development* (Boulder, 2006). Francis Fukuyama's thesis about the end of history, originally made in an essay, was turned into a 1992 book called *The End of History and the Last Man*. The theory of a Thucydides trap was first posited by the great scholar of international relations Graham Allison in a 2012 *Financial Times* essay, though he later expanded upon it in a 2017 book titled *Destined for War: Can America and China Escape Thucydides's Trap?* Finally, Boris Johnson's article 'Africa is a Mess', which has entered the annals of infamy, was published in *The Spectator* in 2002 and can be found on the magazine's website.

8. DEATH OF THE NATION?

Peter Heather's views on the fiscal contract at the heart of the Roman imperial system and of the nature of political integration and dissent within it are explored at greater length in *Rome Resurgent: War and Society in the Age of Justinian* (Oxford, 2017), chs. 1 and 2. There are many wonderful accounts of the Peasants' Revolt, but Rodney Hilton's brilliant *Bond Men*

Made Free: Medieval Peasant Movements and the English Rising of 1381 (London, 1988: in many other editions too) is a great place to begin.

The effect that the rise of the modern periphery has had in reversing the resource flows that helped enrich the West is explored in John Rapley, *Twilight of the Money Gods* (London, 2017). The phenomenon of state erosion giving way to informal types of governance was posited in John Rapley, 'The New Middle Ages', *Foreign Affairs* (2016). On the rise of the global one per cent, and the composition of the top ten per cent, one can do no better than the leading authority, Branko Milanovic, who has published several books on the topic of global inequality, of which the one to start with is *Haves and Have Nots* (New York, 2007). A useful resource is also the annual *Global Wealth Report* put out by Credit Suisse, which allows curious readers to figure out where in the global oligarchy they might fall.

CONCLUSION

The significance of the Byzantine Armada of 468 is explored in more detail in Heather, *The Fall of Rome*, chs. 8 and 9. That it might not have failed is confirmed by the triumphant success of Justinian's expedition of 532: see Heather, *Rome Resurgent*, ch. 5.

Index

migration – *cont'd.*
  imperial collapse and, 3–5,
    104–5, 108–9, 128; *see also*
    Anglo-Saxons, migration into
    Britain and; Barbarian invasion
  imperial expansion and, 23–4,
    30–32, 35, 105–6, 106–11
  NHS (UK) and, 111
  peripheral development and, 38,
    50, 55, 88–90, 97, 99–100,
    107–8, 114
  political discourse (modern) and,
    3–4, 111–12, 148
  policy choices and consequences,
    112–14
  urbanization and, 24
Milan, 34
Mongols, 79
Mosella, poem, 20–21, 32–3
Mossadegh, Mohammed, deposed
  leader of Iran, 54
Mozambique, 119
Mumbai, 114

Nagpur, 44
Narbonne, 93
nation states, 1, 28, 62, 68, 139–41,
    143, 145, 147, 149–51, 153,
    155, 157, 159, 163–4, 167
national debt, 151, 154
National Health Service (UK),
    111, 158
nationalism, 62, 65
  inner peripheries and, 62–8, 74
NATO, 35, 134
neoliberal economics, 117, 120,
    123, 146–7, 157
  globalization and, 117–21, 123,
    144–5, 149–50, 164
Netherlands, 28, 106, 154

New Amsterdam, 28
New France, 47
New York, 28, 70, 72, 126, 143, 147
New Zealand, 9, 47
Nixon, Richard, 53–4
northern Europe, 83, 100, 122
Norway, 113

OECD, 1, 35, 107, 111, 113, 165
offshore havens, 165
OPEC, 117
opium, 43, 129
Orbán, Viktor, 112
Ostrogoths, 79–80, 102
Ottonian Empire, 82

Pakistan, 122, 159, 176
Papua New Guinea, 45
Pavia, 82
Pax Romana, 25, 27
peasants, and revolution, 140–42
pension funds, 121, 148–50, 157
peripheries, imperial, 4–5, 14,
    54–5, 66–8, 85, 88–9, 97,98,
    104, 108, 125, 137, 144,
    149–50, 162–4
  administration in, 63–5, 73–4, 119
  development in, 38–44, 43–52,
    73–4, 82, 83, 114, 116–23,
    127–9, 146–7
  migration and, 120–21
  political consequences of, 56–60,
    62–6, 70–75, 82–4, 90–93,
    115–16, 122–3, 133–5, 137–8,
    166–7
  'inner' and 'outer' distinction,
    41–2, 46, 47–51, 83, 88–90,
    123, 127
  see also imperial systems;
    nationalism